GREAT TRANSITIONS

PREPARING ADOLESCENTS FOR A NEW CENTURY

CONCLUDING REPORT

CARNEGIE COUNCIL ON ADOLESCENT DEVELOPMENT

CARNEGIE CORPORATION OF NEW YORK ■ OCTOBER 1995

Copies of this report may be obtained for $10.00, (single copies, bulk rate available) from: Carnegie Council on Adolescent Development, P.O. Box 753, Waldorf, MD 20604. Telephone (202) 429-7979.

LIBRARY OF CONGRESS CATALOGING-IN-PUBLICATION DATA

Carnegie Council on Adolescent Development.
Great transitions: preparing adolescents for a new century/ concluding report of the Carnegie Council on Adolescent Development.
p.   cm.
ISBN 0-9623154-4-3 (pbk.)
1. Parent and teenager—United States.   2. Teenagers—United States—Attitudes.
3. Social work with teenagers—United States.   4. Teenagers—Health and hygiene
—United States. 5. Adolescent psychology. I. Title.
HQ799.15.C374 1995   95-37472
305.23'5—dc20   cip

Designed and produced by Meadows Design Office Incorporated, Washington, DC
Printed by Graphtec, Inc., Woodlawn, MD

CONTENTS

Adolescence is one of the most fascinating and complex transitions in the life span: a time of accelerated growth and change second only to infancy; a time of expanding horizons, self-discovery, and emerging independence; a time of metamorphosis from childhood to adulthood. Its beginning is associated with biological, physical, behavioral, and social transformations that roughly correspond with the move from elementary school to middle or junior high school. The events of this crucially formative phase can shape an individual's life course and thus the future of the whole society.

Early adolescence, encompassing the sexual awakenings of puberty as well as new social and educational demands, is an age of particular vulnerability. Barely out of childhood, young people ages ten to fourteen are today experiencing more freedom, autonomy, and choice than ever at a time when they still need special nurturing, protection, and guidance. Without the sustained involvement of parents and other adults in safeguarding their welfare, young adolescents are at risk of harming themselves and others.

Many adolescents manage to negotiate their way through this critical transition with relative success. With caring families, good schools, and supportive community institutions, they grow up reasonably well educated, committed to families and friends, and prepared for the workplace and for the responsibilities of citizenship. Even under less-than-optimal conditions for growth and development—the absence of supportive and caring adults, poverty, unsafe schools, and distressed communities—adolescents can become contributing members of society. Some achieve this status despite facing threats to their well-being, such as AIDS and easy access to lethal weapons and drugs, that were all but unknown to their parents and grandparents.

For many others, however, the obstacles in their path can impair their physical and emotional health, destroy their motivation and ability to succeed in school and jobs, and damage their personal relationships. Many reach adulthood ill-equipped to participate responsibly in our democratic society.

Across America today, adolescents are confronting pressures to use alcohol, cigarettes, or other drugs and to have sex at earlier ages. Many are depressed: About a third of adolescents report they have contemplated suicide. Others are growing up lacking the competence to handle interpersonal conflict without resorting to violence. By age seventeen, about a quarter of all adolescents have engaged in behaviors that are harmful or dangerous to themselves and others: getting pregnant, using drugs, taking part in antisocial activity, and failing in school. Altogether, nearly half of American adolescents are at high or moderate risk of seriously damaging their life chances. The damage may be near term and vivid, or it may be delayed, like a time bomb set in youth.

The social and technological changes of this century, and especially of recent decades, have provided many young people with remarkable material benefits and opportunities to master technical skills; they have also introduced new stresses and risks into the adolescent experience. Today, with high divorce rates, increases in both parents working, and the growth of single-parent families, slightly more than half of all American children will spend at least part of their childhood or adolescence living with only one parent. In this situation, exacerbated by the erosion of neighborhood networks and other traditional social support systems, children now spend significantly less time in the company of adults than a few decades ago; more of their time is spent in front of the television set or with their peers in age-segregated, unsupervised environments.

Such conditions occur among families of all income levels and backgrounds and in cities, suburbs, and rural areas. But they are especially severe in neighborhoods of concentrated poverty, where young adolescents are more likely to lack two crucial prerequisites for their healthy growth and development: a close relationship with a dependable adult and the perception of meaningful opportunities in mainstream society.

For today's adolescents, particularly those who do not intend to go beyond high school, there is much less chance to earn a decent living wage, support a family, and participate actively in the life of the community and nation than there was a few decades ago. Many adolescents feel adult-like pressures without experiencing the rewards of belonging and of being useful in the valued settings of adult life. Especially in low-income neighborhoods where good education and jobs are scarce, young people can grow up with a bleak sense of the future.

MEETING THE ESSENTIAL REQUIREMENTS FOR HEALTHY ADOLESCENT DEVELOPMENT

In the face of the social and economic transformations of the late twentieth century, all adolescents have enduring human needs that must be met if they are to grow up to be healthy, constructive adults. All must:

- Find a valued place in a constructive group

- Learn how to form close, durable human relationships

- Feel a sense of worth as a person

- Achieve a reliable basis for making informed choices

- Know how to use the support systems available to them

- Express constructive curiosity and exploratory behavior

- Find ways of being useful to others

- Believe in a promising future with real opportunities

Meeting these requirements has been essential for human survival into adulthood for millennia. But in a technologically advanced democratic society—one that places an increasingly high premium on competence in many domains—adolescents themselves face a further set of challenges. They must:

- Master social skills, including the ability to manage conflict peacefully

- Cultivate the inquiring and problem-solving habits of mind for lifelong learning

- Acquire the technical and analytic capabilities to participate in a world-class economy

- Become ethical persons

- Learn the requirements of responsible citizenship

- Respect diversity in our pluralistic society

Adolescence is the last phase of the life span in which social institutions have reasonably ready access to the entire population, so the potential for constructive influence and for improving adolescents' life chances is great. Early adolescence—the phase during which young people are just beginning to engage in very risky behaviors, but before damaging patterns have become firmly established—offers an excellent opportunity for intervention to prevent later casualties and promote successful adult lives.

ADAPTING PIVOTAL INSTITUTIONS TO FOSTER HEALTHY ADOLESCENCE: GENERIC APPROACHES

The American institutions that have the greatest influence on young adolescents are primarily the family and the schools, but also youth-serving, health-care organizations, and the media. The Carnegie Council on Adolescent Development urges these five institutions to adapt to the impact of a hyper-modern, high-tech, pluralistic society in ways that meet the essential requirements for healthy adolescent development. These institutions have fallen behind in their vital functions and must now be strengthened in their respective roles and linked in a mutually reinforcing system of support for adolescents.

Many current interventions on behalf of young adolescents are targeted to one problem behavior, such as drug abuse or teenage pregnancy. While targeted approaches can be useful, they often do not take adequate account of two important findings from research: (1) serious problem behaviors tend to cluster in the same individual and reinforce one another; and (2) such behaviors often have common antecedents in childhood experience and educational failure. The other side of the coin is that those who engage in healthy lifestyles are more likely to do well in school and to come from supportive family and community structures that reward their effort, promoting self-respect and decent human relations. These observations suggest that families, schools, and other social institutions have a special opportunity—and obligation—to foster healthy lifestyles in childhood and adolescence, taking into consideration the underlying factors that promote either positive or negative outcomes.

The Carnegie Council focuses on approaches that deal with the factors that predispose adolescents to engage in high-risk or problem behaviors. These are *generic* in nature; they are distinguished from categorical or targeted approaches that focus on single problems, often after they have already occurred. Generic approaches focus on the positive possibilities inherent in the adolescent transition—possibilities for educating and motivating young adolescents in the pursuit of healthy lifestyles, for fostering interpersonal and decision-making skills to help them choose alternatives to very risky behavior, and for providing them with reasons and tools to build constructive lives.

Generic approaches that can be adopted by the pivotal institutions include not only strong family relationships and excellent basic education but also a variety of related approaches such as social support networks, adult mentoring, health promotion programs incorporating human biology, peer-mediated services, and life skills training to help young people cope with day-to-day living. If sustained over a period of years, such interventions can offset the negative effects of low self-respect, undeveloped social and decision-making skills, indifference to education, lack of information about health matters, low perception of opportunities, and limited incentives for delaying short-term gratification.

CORE RECOMMENDATIONS

Ensuring the healthy growth and development of adolescents must involve the commitment of all institutions that have a profound impact on youth. No single influence can be responsible for the successful transition from adolescence into adulthood. Families, the schools, the health sector, community organizations, and the media must work singly and in concert to launch all young people on a successful life course. In the twenty-first century, every young person will be essential; no individual will be expendable if our country is to maintain a dynamic, civil society and a flourishing economy in the face of accelerating technological, demographic, and socioeconomic change. The following recommendations of the Carnegie Council offer ways to adapt to the transforming world and provide life chances for adolescents conducive to a better future for the entire society.

REENGAGE FAMILIES WITH THEIR ADOLESCENT CHILDREN

Parental involvement in school activities declines steadily as children progress to middle and high school. Parents need to remain actively engaged in their adolescents' education; schools, for their part, should welcome the families of students as allies and cultivate their support. Schools and other community institutions, including health-care agencies, can help parents deal with the adolescent transition. They can create parent support groups, parent education programs, and education for prospective parents. Employers, both public and private, can pursue more family-friendly policies for parents with young adolescents. Examples are flexible work hours and other measures allowing parents to spend more time with their young adolescents or volunteer in school or youth programs. Under special circumstances, child care tax credits could be extended to parents of young adolescents so they may be enrolled in high-quality after-school programs supervised by responsible, caring adults.

CREATE DEVELOPMENTALLY APPROPRIATE SCHOOLS FOR ADOLESCENTS

States and school districts should give teachers and principals the authority and resources to transform middle schools and junior high schools into health-promoting as well as learning environments—environments that are small-scale and safe, that promote stable relationships between students and their teachers and peers, that are intellectually stimulating, that employ cooperative learning strategies and de-emphasize tracking, that provide health education and life-skills training, and that offer primary health-care services either in or near the school. Schools that are developmentally appropriate provide a core curriculum and teaching methods that excite students' curiosity and build on their desire to explore, strengthen their analytical and problem-solving abilities, and provide an understanding of human biology and its place in the world.

DEVELOP HEALTH-PROMOTION STRATEGIES FOR YOUNG ADOLESCENTS

Poor health interferes with learning; good health facilitates it. Since 1960, the burden of adolescent illness has shifted from the traditional causes of disease to behavior-related problems, such as sexually transmitted diseases, teenage pregnancy, motor vehicle accidents, gun-related homicides and accidents, depression leading to suicide, and abuse of drugs (alcohol and cigarettes as well as illegal drugs). Instilling in adolescents the knowledge, skills, and values that foster physical and mental health will require substantial changes in the way the health professionals work and the way they connect with families, schools, and community organizations. This effort can be facilitated by a conjunction of the life sciences curriculum, life skills training, and social supports for healthy behavior. It will also require filling serious gaps in health services for adolescents. At least three measures are needed to meet these goals. The first is the training and availability of health providers with a deep and sensitive understanding of the developmental needs and behavior-related problems of adolescents. The second is expanded health insurance coverage for adolescents who now experience barriers to these services. The third is increasing school-based and school-related health facilities for adolescents. Taken together, these measures could significantly improve the health outcomes of adolescents.

STRENGTHEN COMMUNITIES WITH YOUNG ADOLESCENTS

Communities should provide more attractive, safe, growth-promoting settings for young adolescents during the out-of-school hours—times of high risk when parents are often not available to supervise their children. More than 17,000 national and local youth organizations, including those sponsored by religious groups, now operate in the United States, but they do not adequately provide opportunities for about one-third of young people who most need their support and guidance. These organizations must now work to expand their reach, enlisting the help of community residents, families, schools, volunteers, and adolescents themselves in offering more activities that convey information about life, careers, and places beyond the neighborhood—as well as engage them in community service and other constructive activities.

PROMOTE THE CONSTRUCTIVE POTENTIAL OF THE MEDIA

An ever-expanding array of media bombard adolescents with messages that powerfully shape their attitudes and behavior. Growing, serious criticism has been directed at television, music media, and video games for their emphasis on violence as the ultimate problem solver and on unrestrained sexuality. The undeniable power of the media could be used far more constructively in the lives of young adolescents. Families, schools, and other pivotal institutions can help young people become more "media literate" so they can examine media messages more critically. They can work with media organizations in developing health-promoting programming and media campaigns for youth. And they can support social actions that discourage the media from glamorizing violence and sex as well as drinking, smoking, and other drug use.

WHAT OTHER INSTITUTIONS CAN DO

Business, universities, scientific and professional organizations, and government at all levels can help pivotal institutions meet the essential requirements of healthy adolescent development.

BUSINESS

The business community can help directly, by providing funds and technical support to implement the recommendations of this report, and indirectly, by mobilizing community leadership on behalf of the education and health of youth. Within the workplace, it can institute family-friendly policies and practices, and it can cooperate in diminishing the production of sex- and violence-saturated media programming.

UNIVERSITIES AND SCIENTIFIC AND PROFESSIONAL ORGANIZATIONS

These "science-rich" institutions and organizations can stimulate interdisciplinary research and publication on the problems and opportunities of adolescent development, recognizing the implications for practice, policy, and social action, and bringing the facts before the public by taking education beyond the campus.

GOVERNMENT

Government at all levels can recognize the critical adolescent years, particularly early adolescence, in its policies and programs and assist communities in translating youth-oriented programs into action. One example is the recent creation of an Office of Adolescent Health in the

U.S. Department of Health and Human Services. That effort, so far, is rudimentary, but it could become a vital focus for healthy adolescent development. Fifteen states are supporting major reforms of middle and junior high schools to make them more developmentally appropriate for young adolescents. More states need to join this movement. Cities and counties can also organize effectively for youth development.

MOBILIZING COMMUNITIES FOR YOUTH

With a combination of informed community leadership and vigorous grass-roots organizing, communities can be mobilized to engage in a strategic planning process on behalf of adolescents and their families, similar to what many communities are today doing to promote a healthy start for newborns. This process can be led by community councils for youth composed of relevant professionals, business and media leaders, local youth organizations, parents, and adolescents themselves. Such councils carefully assess local needs, formulate useful interventions, and inform the entire community about the problems and opportunities of adolescence. Experience thus far has shown that community mobilization is not readily accomplished, but recent constructive examples provide useful guidance.

INVESTING IN OUR FUTURE

Much of the current spending for adolescence could achieve better results if it were redirected toward fundamental, comprehensive approaches. Preventing much of the damage now occurring would have a powerful social and economic impact, including higher productivity, lowered health costs, lowered prison costs, and improved human welfare. In the long run, the vitality of any society and its prospects for the future depend on the quality of its people—on their knowledge and their skill and on the health and the decency of their human relations. In an era when there is much well-founded concern about losing a vital sense of community, these initiatives on behalf of all our children can have profound collateral benefits of building solidarity, mutual aid, civility, and a reasonable basis for hope.

A key lesson learned from the Council's experience is the importance of serious, careful examination of the facts, nonpartisan analyses, broad dissemination with involvement of key sectors, and sustained commitment over a period of years. Above all, a long-term view is essential to bring about the difficult, indeed fundamental, changes necessary in modern society to improve the life chances of all our children.

■ ■ ■ ■ ■ ■ ■ ■

PART I

Great Transitions

LAND OF DIMINISHING DREAMS

The year is two thousand fifty-four,
The world is full of curses.
People walk the streets no more,
No women carry purses.

The name of the game is survival now—
Safety is far in the past.
Families are huge, with tons of kids
In hopes that one will last.

Drugs are no longer looked down upon,
They are a way of life.
They help us escape the wrenching stress
Of our fast world's endless strife . . .

I wake up now—it was only a dream,
But the message was terribly clear.
We'd better think hard about the future
Before our goals and our dreams disappear.

JESSICA INGLIS, 16

CHAPTER ONE

Early Adolescence: The Great Transition

Adolescence is one of the most fascinating and complex transitions in the life span: a time of accelerated growth and change second only to infancy; a time of expanding horizons, self-discovery, and emerging independence; a time of metamorphosis from childhood to adulthood. Its beginning is associated with biological, physical, behavioral, and social transformations that roughly correspond with the move to middle or junior high school. The events of this crucially formative phase can shape an individual's entire life course and thus the future of the whole society.

In these often tumultuous years, a young person experiences much growth and joy, some anxiety and dread. Relationships with peers and family take on new meaning. Doubt and confusion abound. Some young people believe they can see into their future and find nothing to hope for. Others dream but often have no more than a vague image of the future as they embark on a prolonged search for the pathways to promising adulthood.

In societies everywhere, the onset of adolescence is closely synchronized with the biological changes of puberty. In most technologically advanced countries today, puberty begins on average two years earlier than it did a century ago, and the transition to adulthood can last a decade or more. In the United States, adolescence now extends over so many years that it can be usefully subdivided into several phases. *Early adolescence*, encompassing the changes of puberty as well as sexual and psychological awakenings, extends roughly from ages ten through fourteen. *Middle adolescence*, a time of increased autonomy and experimentation, covers ages fifteen to seventeen. *Late adolescence*, occurring for those who delay their entry into adult roles because of educational or social factors, can stretch from age eighteen into the twenties.

The distinction between early and late adolescence can be illustrated by comparing eleven- and twelve-year-olds to seventeen- and eighteen-year-olds. They have very little in common with each other. Young adolescents are barely out of childhood and, much like younger children, still need special nurturing and protection; older adolescents share many of the attributes of adults.

Many young people manage to negotiate their way through the critical adolescent years with relative ease. With good schools, caring families, and supportive community institutions, they grow into adulthood well educated, committed to families and friends, and prepared for the workplace and the responsibilities of citizenship. Even under less-than-optimal conditions for growth and development, many become contributing members of society.[2] Some achieve this status despite having faced threats to their well-being (such as AIDS and easy access to guns) that were all but unknown to their parents and grandparents.

For others, however, the obstacles in their path can impair their physical and emotional health, destroy their motivation and ability to succeed in school and jobs, and damage personal relationships. Many are at high risk of reaching adulthood ill-equipped to participate responsibly in our democratic society.[3]

Both groups of adolescents—those who appear to be making a reasonably successful transition to adulthood and those for whom meaningful options may seem closed by the age of fourteen or fifteen—are the urgent concern of the Carnegie Council on Adolescent Development, established in 1986 as a program of Carnegie Corporation of New York. Since 1987, the Council has worked to generate broad-based understanding of this vulnerable age group. Composed of national leaders from education, law, science, health, religion, business, the media, youth-serving agencies, and government, the Council has sought to synthesize the best available knowledge and experience about adolescence in America and to stimulate public and private interest in facilitating the transition from adolescence to adulthood. Ultimately, the Council's mission has been to place the challenges of the adolescent years higher on the nation's agenda. In the 1990s, it also has sought to stimulate interest in this critical transition as it occurs in other countries.

WHY EARLY ADOLESCENCE?

In its work, the Council has focused attention on the challenges of early adolescence, ages ten to fourteen. Important in its own right as a potentially rewarding time of personal growth and development, it is the age in which individuals adopt behavior patterns in education and health that can have lifelong significance. For this reason, early adolescence presents a vital opportunity for shaping enduring patterns of behavior that can set a young person on a successful course for life.[4]

Until recently, early adolescence was neglected in scientific inquiry, in policy formation, and in public understanding. Within the scientific and professional practice communities, however, a notable consensus has begun to emerge on new ways of viewing the risks and opportunities inherent in the early adolescent transition. This consensus is based on a growing body of research and practical experience regarding adolescent health, education, and development.[5]

The new view asserts that early adolescence is part of a developmental continuum, profoundly shaped by practices and policies that affect young people both before and after this period. It reflects recent research strongly suggesting that the problems that impair learning and health tend to cluster in individual adolescents[6] and that the behavior patterns associated with these problems often have common antecedents in childhood experiences and in educational failure.[7]

Such a view of early adolescence requires that those responsible for policies and programs affecting adolescents take a broad approach to the promotion of health and the prevention of high-risk behavior. Typically, policymakers have adopted categorical approaches to single problems without seeking to coordinate these approaches. The Council believes that more effective solutions can be found if those responsible for nurturing adolescents build a supportive and caring infrastructure for adolescents composed of several pivotal institutions working in concert to meet the fundamental requirements for healthy development.[8]

No one institution in isolation can ensure that today's adolescents will grow into responsible, decent, thoughtful, and competent adults. Rather, it is the mutual influence of these institutions that will be critical. Together, they have the potential to address the underlying factors that increase the likelihood of millions of young people becoming involved in serious health-compromising behaviors. The approaches to the myriad problems of adolescents at risk presented here can be adapted for use in a variety of settings.

In the Council's view of adolescence, all adolescents must meet the same fundamental requirements if they are to be prepared for success in adulthood. They must find ways to earn respect, establish a sense of belonging to one or more highly valued groups, make close and enduring human relationships, and build a sense of personal worth based on useful skills. They must learn, in our pluralistic society, to live peacefully and respectfully with a wide array of ethnic, religious, and cultural groups. They must have the help of caring adults to develop a positive vision of the future, to see images of what adulthood offers and requires, and to prepare themselves for opportunities that are available to them. With appropriate guidance and support from families, schools, and other institutions, young people can grow up with the skills and values needed to participate in a humane, civil society.

The social and economic costs of adverse circumstances that distort adolescent development are unacceptable. They encompass not only personal tragedies, but also widespread disease and disability, ignorance and incompetence, crime and violence, alienation and hatred. Such tragedies are not confined in any tidy way to certain geographic areas or specific groups. Like a toxin, they poison the environment and do wide-ranging harm throughout the nation.

Although disturbing numbers of today's young adolescents face tremendous odds, there is not the slightest reason to believe that they are less talented or resourceful than were their predecessors. The difference is their transformed circumstances, which are creating unprecedented challenges for them. To help young adolescents learn what they must to survive and flourish, we have to understand these changed circumstances and new challenges better. Such understanding can contribute to formulating useful strategies for helping young adolescents cope with a world that itself is in the process of transformation.

The United States is a large, heterogeneous, multiethnic nation with a strong tradition of individualism. These are significant assets, but they also make it difficult for Americans to arrive at a shared understanding of complicated social problems and to turn that understanding into solutions that can win broad acceptance. Can we envision how schools, churches, families, businesses, youth organizations, health-care agencies, the media, organizations of the scientific

> The problems of adolescence deal with deep and moving human experiences. They center on a fateful time in the life course when poorly informed decisions can have lifelong consequences. The tortuous passage from childhood to adulthood requires our highest attention, our understanding, and a new level of thoughtful commitment.[1]
>
> **DAVID A. HAMBURG, PRESIDENT**
> **CARNEGIE CORPORATION OF NEW YORK**

community, and government can cooperate in addressing the developmental needs of youth? Reaching a consensus on the values and behaviors appropriate for adolescents and on the steps that can be taken to help young people make a successful transition to adulthood will certainly be arduous. But we must try, for it is not only the lives of young people that are at stake: it is also our common future.

THE REPORT'S PERSPECTIVE

Great Transitions: Preparing Adolescents for a New Century, the Carnegie Council's concluding report, draws together the findings and analyses from its decade-long efforts on behalf of young adolescents. In doing so, the report presents for the first time the Council's distinctive view of adolescence and of the steps our nation must take to ensure each adolescent's safe passage into adulthood. Although the focus is on early adolescence, the concepts for the most part apply to middle adolescence as well, as reflected in some of the data and examples.

Much of the material for this report has been drawn from the Council's published reports, syntheses of research, and working papers, all of which were prepared with the guidance of the Council members and with support from Carnegie Corporation of New York. This body of work (see the appendices for a complete listing) includes the Council's first major report, *Turning Points: Preparing American Youth for the 21st Century* (1989); *At the Threshold: The Developing Adolescent* (1990); *Life Skills Training: Preventive Interventions for Young Adolescents* (1990); *School and Community Support Programs that Enhance Adolescent Health and Education* (1990); *A Matter of Time: Risk and Opportunity in the Nonschool Hours* (1992); *Fateful Choices: Healthy Youth for the 21st Century* (1992); and *Promoting the Health of Adolescents: New Directions for the Twenty-first Century* (1993). This concluding report also considers important aspects of adolescent development addressed in other Council publications, meetings, and cooperative efforts. One of these is a three-volume publication of the U.S. Congress's Office of Technology Assessment, *Adolescent Health* (1991).[9]

The Council's approach to fostering healthy development during adolescence and beyond takes into account scientific knowledge about adolescents and identifies factors that will enable adolescents to meet developmental challenges successfully. This approach rests on six basic concepts about adolescence:

- **Early adolescence is a critical turning point in life's trajectory.** This period, therefore, represents an optimal time for interventions to prevent destructive behavior and promote enduring healthful practices.

- **Education and health are inextricably related.** Adolescents have difficulty learning when they are not in good health. Good health during adolescence facilitates learning, with powerful lifelong effects. By the same token, education constitutes one of the most powerful influences on health through the entire life span.[10]

- **Destructive, or health-damaging, behaviors in adolescence tend to cluster.** Positive, or health-promoting, behaviors also tend to cluster.[11]

- **Common underlying factors contribute to many problem behaviors in adolescents.** One is academic difficulty; another is the absence of strong and sustained guidance from caring adults.[12]

- **Preventive interventions are more likely to be successful if they address the underlying factors that contribute to problem behaviors.**

- **Given the complexity of influences on adolescents, the essential requirements for healthy, positive development must be met through the joint efforts of a set of pivotal institutions that powerfully affect adolescents' experiences.** These pivotal institutions begin with the family and include schools as well as a wide array of neighborhood and community organizations.

Based on these six concepts, the Council's recommendations for change take into account the many factors that influence learning and health, both in and out of school. If the recommendations in this report are fully implemented, the institutions of society that most influence the development of adolescents will be strengthened to foster healthy choices among adolescents—choices that can make the difference between the fulfillment of aspiration or the eclipse of hope.

■ ■ ■ ■ ■ ■ ■ ■

Young Adolescents Face Serious Risks

In 1993, approximately 7.3 percent (19 million) of the U.S. population were young adolescents, ages ten to fourteen. Of these, approximately 20 percent were living below the federal poverty line, which in 1993 was $14,763 for a family of four. Minority adolescents were disproportionately poor: 43 percent of African American adolescents and 38 percent of Hispanic/Latino adolescents lived in poverty, compared with 15 percent of white adolescents. By the year 2000, more than one-third of all young adolescents will be members of racial or ethnic minorities: African Americans (16 percent); American Indian, Eskimo, and Aleut (1 percent), Asian/Pacific Americans (5 percent), and Hispanic/Latino (14 percent).[1] To compete in the global economy of the twenty-first century, America will need all of these young people to be healthy and well educated.

HEALTH RISKS

- Injuries are the leading cause of death for young adolescents. The largest single cause of death among these adolescents is injuries from motor vehicle crashes.[2]

- The firearm homicide rate for ten- to fourteen-year-olds more than doubled between 1985 and 1992 (from 0.8 to 1.9 per 100,000). For black males, the rate increased from 3.0 to 8.4 per 100,000 during the same period.[3]

- In 1992, twelve- to fifteen-year-olds had a high overall victimization rate. They were victims of assault more than any other age group.[4]

- In a national representative sample of adolescents ten to sixteen years old, one-fourth of respondents reported having experienced an assault or abuse in the previous year.[5] Approximately 20 percent of the documented child abuse and neglect cases in 1992 involved young adolescents between the ages of ten and thirteen years.[6]

- Use of alcohol and cigarettes remains more widespread than use of illegal drugs.

- Although it is illegal to sell alcohol to individuals under twenty-one years of age, two-thirds of eighth graders report that they have already tried alcohol and a quarter say that they are current drinkers. Twenty-eight percent of eighth graders say that they have been drunk at least once.[7]

- Among eighth graders, who are thirteen to fourteen years old, the rate of current smoking (smoking any cigarette in the past 30 days) rose by 30 percent between 1991 and 1994, from 14.3 to 18.6 percent.[8]

- Marijuana use among eighth graders more than doubled between 1991 and 1994 from 6.2 to 13.0 percent.[9]

- Over the last three decades, the age of first intercourse has declined. Higher proportions of adolescent women and men reported being sexually experienced at each age between the ages of fifteen and twenty in 1988 than in the early 1970s. In 1988, 27 percent of girls and 33 percent of boys had intercourse by their fifteenth birthday.[10]

- While the number of births to those ages fifteen and younger is not large, this group is experiencing the greatest rate of increased births. Pregnancy rates for all girls younger than fifteen years old rose 4.1 percent in the United States during the period between 1980 and 1988—higher than any other teenage group.[11]

- Current evidence indicates that increases in depressive disorders and mood swings are greater for girls than for boys during adolescence. By age fourteen to fifteen, girls are twice as likely as boys to suffer from depression, a gender difference that persists into adulthood.

- From 1980 to 1992, the rate of suicide among young adolescents increased 120 percent and increased most dramatically among young black males (300 percent) and young white females (233 percent). Suicide rates for ten- to fourteen-year- old American Indians are four times higher than those for ten- to fourteen-year- olds of all races.[12]

EDUCATIONAL RISKS

- The average proficiency in science, mathematics, and writing among thirteen-year-olds was slightly higher in 1992 than it was in the 1970s. However, these achievements have not improved enough to keep pace with the higher level of skills required in a global economy.[13]

- Only 28 percent of eighth graders scored at or above the proficiency level in reading in 1994. Two percent read at or above an advanced level.[14]

- In 1990, 7 percent of the eighth-grade class of 1988 (most of whom were then fifteen and sixteen years old) were dropouts.[15] By their senior year (1992), 12 percent of this class were dropouts.[16] Dropout rates vary by students' race/ethnicity: white (9.4); black (14.5); Hispanic (18.3); Asian/Pacific Islanders (7.0); and American Indian (25.4).[17]

SOURCES

1. Day, J. C. (1993). *Population projections of the United States by age, sex, race, and hispanic origin: 1993–2050.* U.S. Bureau of the Census, Current Population Reports. Washington, DC: U.S. Government Printing Office.

2. National Center for Health Statistics, Unpublished data, 1994.

3. Ibid.

4. Bureau of Justice Statistics. (1994). *Criminal victimization in the United States, 1992.* NCJ-145125. Washington, DC: U.S. Government Printing Office.

5. Finkelhor, D., & Dziuba-Leatherman, J. (1994). Children as victims of violence: A national survey. *Pediatrics 94*:413–420.

6. U.S. Bureau of the Census. (1994). *Statistical abstract of the United States, 1994* (114th edition). Washington, DC: U.S. Government Printing Office.

7. Johnston, L. D., O'Malley, P. M., & Bachman, J. G. (1994). *National survey results on drug use from the Monitoring the Future study, 1975–1993, volume I, secondary school students.* Rockville, MD: National Institute on Drug Abuse.

8. Johnston, L. D., O'Malley, P. M., & Bachman, J. G. (1995). *National survey results on drug use from the Monitoring the Future study, 1975–1994.* Rockville, MD: National Institute on Drug Abuse.

9. Johnston, L. D., O'Malley, P. M.., & Bachman, J. G., 1994.

10. The Alan Guttmacher Institute. (1994). *Sex and America's teenagers.* New York: Author.

11. U.S. General Accounting Office. (1995). *Welfare dependency: Coordinated community efforts can better serve young at-risk teen girls.* GAO/HEHS/RCED-95–108. Washington, DC: Author.

12. Morbidity and Mortality Weekly Report. Suicide among children, adolescents, and young adults—United States, 1980–1992. Vol. 44, No. 15, April 21, 1995; and U.S. Congress, Office of Technology Assessment. (1990). *Indian adolescent mental health* (OTA-H-446). Washington, DC: U.S. Government Printing Office.

13. U.S. Department of Education, National Center for Education Statistics, "1994 NAEP reading: A first look." April 1995.

14. Ibid.

15. They were not enrolled in school and had not finished high school.

16. U.S Department of Education, 1995.

17. National Center for Education Statistics. (1994). *The condition of education, 1994.* NCES94–149. Washington, DC: U.S. Government Printing Office.

CHAPTER TWO

Growing Up in Early Adolescence: An Emerging View

For all young people, adolescence involves a daunting array of interrelated developmental challenges: the biological changes of puberty with their meaning for reproductive capacity and new social roles; the handling of feelings of sexual arousal in situations that demand the postponement of sexual behavior; the move toward psychological and physical independence from parents; the search for friendship and belonging among peers; the negotiation of new and conflicting demands and pressures; the exploration of novel ideas and risky behavior; the engagement in more complex intellectual tasks; and the formulation of a distinct identity.

Substantial progress has been made through research in capturing the complexity of adolescence and in determining the common features of adolescent experiences.[1] As a result, we now understand how adolescents navigate the transition from childhood to adulthood, how development can go wrong even in affluent circumstances, and how those in less advantaged circumstances, especially from areas of concentrated poverty, succeed or succumb.[2]

New knowledge about adolescence has begun to illuminate the positive and adaptive qualities of this transitional stage in development as well as the problems.[3] Although young adolescents are often stereotyped as moody, rebellious, self-indulgent, and incapable of learning anything serious, research indicates that this portrait is greatly overdrawn. Young adolescents are also, at this time, full of curiosity, imagination, and emerging idealism. For many, adolescence is a time of remarkable psychological and social growth that offers excitement and hope, if sometimes anguish and disappointment.

Although much is still unexamined and further research is greatly needed, the emergent view directly challenges the predominantly negative connotations of the term "adolescent." Several important findings challenge prevailing stereotypes about adolescents.

- **Adolescents are a heterogeneous group.** Adolescents are a far-from-monolithic group. On the contrary, they vary greatly in their physical development, life experiences, values, and aspirations.[4] Even individuals of the same age differ enormously in their growth patterns, personalities, aptitudes, and coping skills. Some move into adult roles as early as age fifteen or sixteen, particularly if they are from low-income or working-class backgrounds. Others, especially those born into relative affluence, engage in a protracted period of search and discovery, sorting out their sense of identity, their career directions, and their expectations of adult life before making critical decisions.

  Puberty, which opens the door to adolescence, also varies from person to person.[5] Puberty begins in some individuals as early as age eight and in others as late as age fourteen, making a difference in their self-image, expectations, experiences in school, and relationships with peers and adults.

- **Social, environmental, and hormonal factors are all important in shaping development.** It is widely believed that pubescent adolescents are prey to "raging hormones," with the implication that they are out of control and that little can be done to influence them. The drastic changes in secretion of sex hormones during early adolescence do have profound effects on every tissue of the body—most notably the reproductive system but also the brain. These hormones produce the growth spurt, secondary sex characteristics, and feelings of sexual arousal. They also herald an increase in emotional intensity, with girls experiencing more depression[6] and boys experiencing more aggression. But these changes do not mean that young adolescents are inherently difficult, contrary, or uneducable. The effects of these changes are highly influenced by social and interpersonal factors. When such influences are positive, the biological transition goes more smoothly.[7]

- **Youth culture is different from that of adults but not necessarily in opposition to adult values.** The social organization of adolescents is distinct from that of the child or the adult, with its own music, heroes and heroines, language, and styles. Within this society, there are adolescent subgroups, each emphasizing particular interests, attitudes, and values.[8] But youth culture is not essentially oppositional or hostile to adults. Many adolescents report that they continue to consult with their parents on matters of concern to them, and many relate well to adults other than their parents.[9] Although tensions are inevitable in this time of major transition, only a minority of teenagers engages in rebellion against their parents as they seek to establish a sense of autonomy and separate identity. The process of moving away from parental authority usually leads not to estrangement but to a renegotiated interdependence with family and kin.[10]

- **Peer influence among adolescents may be positive as well as negative.** Despite negative stereotypes, the influence of peers often is beneficial to adolescents.[11] In favorable circumstances, adolescents feel secure with their friends, find joy in the group, and acquire a basis for hope. Peers can contribute to a young person's self-esteem, sense of identity, and achievement. If a young teen becomes solidly established in a constructive peer network—one oriented to study and learning, good health, and decent human relations—the chances are enhanced that he or she will evolve into an inquiring and problem-solving, caring individual.

- **Adolescents are capable of complex reasoning, including the weighing of consequences.** Research has shown that the capacity for critical thinking and for competent decision making is achieved or achievable by early to middle adolescence.[12] For young adolescents, yielding the certainty of childhood is accompanied by a new appreciation of the relativity and complexity of knowledge and ideas. Unfortunately, many school systems do a profound disservice to young adolescents by withholding challenging instruction from them. Educators have a great opportunity to capture the young person's emergent sense of self and curiosity about the world.

Along with their growing capacity for thinking and decision making, adolescents have enhanced opportunities for self-determination in many areas of their lives. They have more control, for example, over how vigorously they apply themselves in school, the kinds of friends they have of both genders, and the extent to which they adopt or avoid such perilous behavior as smoking, using alcohol or other harmful drugs, and engaging in early or promiscuous sexual activity. Unfortunately, the tendency of young adolescents to focus on the here and now rather than on the long-range consequences of their actions places them in substantial danger of making serious errors of judgment.

> One-third of American adolescents today are of non-European descent from a wide array of religious, ethnic, and national backgrounds. . . . Learning to live peacefully while respecting diversity will be a major task for adults in the twenty-first century.

ADOLESCENT ATTRIBUTES OFFER OPPORTUNITIES

Certain characteristics of this period of life make possible adaptive responses to the challenge of major change. If the pivotal institutions that influence adolescents can harness these characteristics, they can provide adolescents with a crucial advantage, enabling them not only to survive but also to thrive under the extraordinary dislocations of contemporary society. Three characteristics are especially significant.

- **Adolescents are eager for authoritative information.** Young adolescents are interested in and receptive to information about themselves and their bodies.[13] In earlier times, their world view and much of the information available to them was shaped by the nuclear and extended family and older peers. Today, information conveyed to adolescents comes largely from the media and peers. Much of it is incorrect or misleading or embodies values that are inimical to young people's self-image and health. Yet the eagerness of these young people for information relevant to their development is a fundamental asset, and pivotal institutions can respond in many constructive and helpful ways.

■ **Adolescents are explorers of the unknown.** Much exploration by adolescents is developmentally appropriate and socially adaptive, even though it can introduce new demands and generate new conflicts. Adolescents ask many questions about themselves and the world—questions that constitute stepping stones across the rapids between childhood and adult life. What is happening? Is it interesting? Is it fun? Does it lead anywhere? What can I do to be better liked? What can I do to be smarter, stronger, better looking? What kind of person am I anyway? Does anyone care about me? What do I really care about? Can I make a difference? How does school relate to the rest of my life? What kind of work do I want to do? How do I give myself a good future? Families, friends, schools, community organizations, religious institutions, health care providers, and the media have a serious responsibility to deal respectfully with the questions that preoccupy teenagers.

■ **Adolescents are strongly influenced by what they see of adult behavior as they "try on" their eventual roles as adults.** At this time of life, a young adolescent is confronted with multiple concepts of what it means to be an adult. Older peers, who are looked up to as having links to the adult world, play an important role as young adolescents select among these images. Some will conclude that it is grown-up to be cool and reject education, to live for the moment, to take what they can get without respect for others, to get high on alcohol or other drugs, to be tough, unyielding, even violent. Such damaging concepts of adulthood are available in abundance in the social environment of young adolescents. But there are also positive, enriching images available that can influence the choices and decisions that young people make.

To help adolescents meet the challenges of adulthood in a changing world that is growing ever more complex, adults in key institutions must respond to make the best use of these positive and adaptive qualities of adolescents. Right now, the vulnerability of young adolescents to health and educational risks is far greater than most people are aware of, and the casualties are mounting. The following chapter will clarify the economic and social consequences of preventable damage and the sadly lost potential of youth in the context of ongoing transformation. Tragedies are not inevitable. Using the guidance provided by the new research on adolescence, the leadership of key institutions throughout society can take steps to intervene in young lives during the pivotal moment of early adolescence. Small steps, taken at this critical time of life, can make a big difference in determining an adolescent's life chances.

> New knowledge about adolescence has begun to illuminate the positive and adaptive qualities of this transitional stage in development as well as the problems. Although young adolescents are often stereotyped as moody, rebellious, self-indulgent, and incapable of learning anything serious, research indicates that this portrait is greatly overdrawn.

Further Reading

Feldman, S.S., & Elliott, G.R. (Eds.). (1990). *At the threshold: The developing adolescent.* Cambridge, MA: Harvard University Press.

Hamburg, B.A. (1974). Early adolescence: A specific and stressful stage of the life cycle. In G.V. Coelho, D.A. Hamburg, & J.E. Adams (Eds.), *Coping and adaptation* (pp. 101–124). New York: Basic Books.

Hamburg, D.A. (1989). *Early adolescence: A critical time for interventions in education and health.* Presidential Essay reprinted from 1989 Annual Report of Carnegie Corporation of New York.

Lerner, R. M. (Ed.). (1993). *Early adolescence: Perspectives on research, policy, and intervention.* Hillsdale, NJ: Lawrence Erlbaum Associates.

Economic Consequences of Preventable Problems

Adolescent pregnancy and substance abuse are not simply problems when they happen. The consequences of these acts reach far into the future, and their antecedents emerge even before adolescence. The following costs illustrate the importance of preventing such problems.

DROPPING OUT

- Remaining in school is the single most important action adolescents can take to improve their future economic prospects. In 1992, a high school graduate earned almost $6,000 per year more than a high school dropout.[1]

- Going to college boosts income even more. In 1992, college graduates had a mean annual income of $32,629, while high school graduates had a mean annual income of $18,737. Earning a professional degree added $40,000 a year to the mean annual income of college graduates.[1]

- Gender also affects income. A male high school graduate's mean monthly income is likely to be twice as much as a female high school graduate's, a statistic that highlights the significance of education for women.[2]

BEARING CHILDREN

- Women who become mothers as teenagers are more likely to find themselves living in poverty later in their lives than women who delay childbearing. Although 28 percent of women who gave birth as teenagers were poor in their 20s and 30s, only 7 percent of women who gave birth after adolescence were living in poverty in their 20s and 30s.[3]

- In 1992, the federal government spent nearly $34 billion on Aid to Families with Dependent Children, Medicaid, and food stamps for families begun by adolescents.[4]

- Providing family planning services is one way to lower taxpayers' costs. Each public dollar spent on family planning services saves an average of $4.40 by reducing expenditures on medical, welfare, and nutritional programs.[5]

SUBSTANCE USE AND ABUSE

- Substance abuse costs the United States more than $238 billion a year, including the expense of treating substance abuse, the productivity losses caused by premature death and inability to perform usual activities, and costs related to crime, destruction of property, and other losses.[6]

- Each year more than a million young people start smoking regularly, a decision that will cost the health care system $8.2 billion in preventable medical expenditures during their lifetimes.[7]

- During the last two decades, the tobacco industry has dramatically increased the money it spends on advertising. In 1992, the industry spent more than $5.2 billion on advertising, making cigarettes second only to automobiles in advertising dollars spent.[8]

INJURIES

- An estimated 10 to 20 percent of all injuries to children and young people occur in and around schools. Falls were the most common cause of injuries. Representing 46 percent of all incidents, falls were followed by sports activities at 30 percent and assaults at 10 percent. The resulting costs of these injuries vary substantially. The bill for treating something as simple as a forearm fracture, for example, can exceed $3,900. A serious injury such as spinal cord damage can incur medical costs higher than $188,000.[9]

- Injuries to young adolescents, ages ten to fifteen, in motor vehicles cost more than $13 million in 1991, or about $56,000 per injured child.[10]

- The U.S. Centers for Disease Control and Prevention estimates that simply switching to break-away bases for softball games could prevent 1.7 million injuries a year and save $2 billion in acute medical costs.[11]

- A recent U.S. Government Accounting Office report estimated that the nation's schools need $112 billion to complete all of the repairs, renovations, and modernizations required to restore facilities to good overall condition and comply with federal mandates that ensure the safety of students.[12]

VIOLENCE

- Violence is a social problem with tremendous economic costs. In 1993, the cost of providing emergency transportation, medical care, hospital stays, rehabilitation, and related treatment for American firearm victims ages 10 through 19 was $407 million.[13]

SOURCES

1. U.S. Department of Commerce, Bureau of the Census. (1994). More education means higher career earnings. *Statistical Brief* SB/94–17. Washington, DC: Author.

2. U.S. Bureau of the Census. (1994). *Statistical abstract of the United States: 1994*. (114th edition). Washington, DC: U.S. Government Printing Office.

3. Alan Guttmacher Institute. (1994). *Sex and America's teenagers*. New York: Author.

4. U.S. Government Accounting Office. (May 1995). *Welfare dependency: Coordinated community efforts can better serve young at-risk teen girls*. RCED-95-108. Washington, DC: Author.

5. Teenage pregnancy and birth rates—United States, 1990. (1990). *Morbidity and Mortality Weekly Report*. October 1, 1993, *42* (38): 733–737.

6. Institute for Health Policy. (1993). *Substance abuse: The nation's number one health problem: Key indicators for health policy*. Waltham, MA: Author.

7. Lynch, B. S., & Bonnie, R. J. (1994). *Growing up tobacco free: Preventing nicotine addiction in children and youths*. Washington, DC: National Academy Press.

8. Federal Trade Commission. (1992). *Report to Congress pursuant to the federal Cigarette Labeling and Advertising Act*. In remarks by David A. Kessler. The Samuel Rubin Program at the Columbia University School of Law, March 8, 1995.

9. Children's Safety Network. (1994). *Injuries in the environment: A resource packet*. Newton, MA: Author.

10. Children's Safety Network Economics and Insurance Resource Center, National Public Services Research Institute. (1992). *Child Occupant Injury Facts*. Landover, MD

11. National Institutes of Health. (1992). *Sport injuries in youth: Surveillance strategies*. NIH Publication No. 93–3444. Washington, DC: U.S. Government Printing Office.

12. U.S. General Accounting Office. (1995). *School facilities: Condition of America's schools*. HEHS-95-61. Washington, DC: Author.

13. Miller, T. (1995). Children's Safety Network Economics and Insurance Resource Center, and National Public Services Research Institute. Unpublished data.

CHAPTER THREE

Old Biology in New Circumstances: The Changing Adolescent Experience

The biology of puberty in today's adolescent is essentially the same as it always has been. Triggered by events in the brain, the pituitary gland produces hormones that stimulate the secretion of sex hormones. These hormones, in turn, have powerful effects on many tissues of the body, including the brain, and lead to significant changes in social, emotional, and sexual behavior.

In modern, complex societies such as the United States, however, the social context for this biological series of events has changed dramatically. Industrialization, urbanization, technological advances, geographic mobility, and cultural diversity have radically transformed the human environment. The interaction between the old biology and this new environment, in turn, has fundamentally altered the conditions for growing up as an adolescent in America.

The swiftness of this change, in historical terms, challenges our understanding and the capacity of our key socializing institutions to adapt to meet new needs. As a result, many families and their adolescents are not faring as well as they should. The often startling statistics on negative events during adolescence (e.g., school-age pregnancy, crime and violence, poor achievement in school, and disability and death because of risky health behaviors) cross boundaries of socioeconomic status, ethnicity, and neighborhood.

THE CHANGED CONTEXT FOR DEVELOPING ADOLESCENTS

The essence of human survival is the ability to adapt to the changing environment. In earlier generations, the transition from childhood to adulthood was gradual and cumulative. Despite generally greater vulnerability to the vicissitudes of nature, children mainly grew up in the context of a cohesive family and a small community with shared values and relatively slow technological and social change. In such an environment, adolescents could count on authoritative information, adult guidance, and social stability.

Adolescents spent most of their time in the presence of adults. Young people worked on family-based farms or in small businesses and youth apprenticeships. Most adolescents' leisure time was spent in the homes of their families and neighbors. Except in large cities, adolescents' social contacts were largely limited to near neighbors. It was scarcely possible for a "youth culture" to develop, except for gangs in some big cities.

In earlier times, children observed their elders closely and learned by so doing. The tasks they were given from an early age pointed toward their future responsibilities. These tasks increased in scope and complexity as the children grew up; valued skills were developed step by step. When they reached adolescence, young people were familiar with what they would have to do as adults and what their opportunities would be. Adults controlled the sexuality and reproduction of the young by arranging marriages soon after girls reached puberty. With dowries, parents often helped provide the economic basis for the start of a new family.

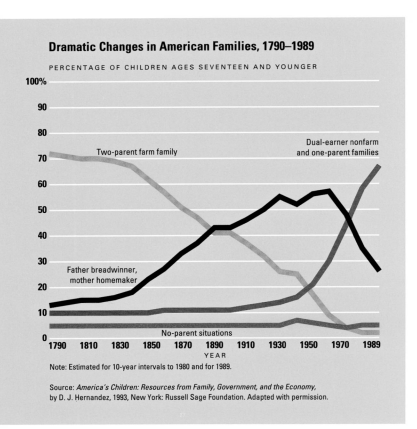

Dramatic Changes in American Families, 1790–1989

PERCENTAGE OF CHILDREN AGES SEVENTEEN AND YOUNGER

Two-parent farm family

Dual-earner nonfarm and one-parent families

Father breadwinner, mother homemaker

No-parent situations

YEAR

Note: Estimated for 10-year intervals to 1980 and for 1989.

Source: *America's Children: Resources from Family, Government, and the Economy,* by D. J. Hernandez, 1993, New York: Russell Sage Foundation. Adapted with permission.

The changes of this century, and especially of recent decades, have provided most children with remarkable material benefits as well as opportunities to master many skills; but they have also brought with them major dislocations of families, communities, and the economy and thus introduced new stresses into the adolescent experience. Consequently, many adolescents now must navigate these treacherous transitional years with fewer social supports and with far less guidance than was formerly available. Among the most significant transformations influencing adolescent development today are the following:

- **Dramatic Changes in American Families.** As kinship and neighborhood networks have steadily eroded and divorce has become common, family life has splintered. Today, slightly more than half of all American children will spend at least part of their childhood or adolescence in a single-parent family—a much higher proportion than a few decades ago.[1] By age sixteen, close to half of the adolescent children of married parents will have seen their parents divorce or marry again.[2] Remarriage presents children with the task of managing multiple family ties and disruptions in family relationships.

- **Less Time Spent with Adults.** With the growth of two-worker families and the geographic dispersal of the extended family, adolescents are spending much of their time with peers in age-segregated environments. Although there has been less research than the problem deserves, the time that American children spend with their parents has decreased significantly in the past few decades.[3] A 1988 survey found that about 27 percent of eighth graders spent two or more hours at home alone after school.[4] Unsupervised afterschool hours represent a period of significant risk for engaging in substance abuse and sexual activity.[5]

- **Changing Structure of Work.** Economic restructuring and the globalization of the marketplace have occurred so rapidly that unskilled individuals can find only low-paying work, often with little prospect of improvement. Entire adequate wage/low-skills industries have virtually disappeared in recent years. High school graduates who do not go on to postsecondary education are typically relegated to low-status, dead-end jobs.[6] The growing disparity in incomes between the economically advantaged and the poor[7] constitutes a threat to the prospects and morale of many adolescents and their parents. The material deprivation and job loss that interfere with effective parenting under conditions of poverty can give young people a bleak sense of the future.

- **Earlier Reproductive Capacity Yet Later Marriage and Work.** The hiatus between the advent of reproductive capacity in individuals and their attainment of independent adult status has lengthened.[8] Infection control and better nutrition in developed countries have lowered the average age at which menstruation begins to twelve and a half. At the same time, the period required for education and training and for achieving stable, productive employment has increased and marriages occur later. For many adolescents, there are few meaningful opportunities to participate directly in the adult world and in community life. Many, therefore, are uncertain how to be useful and earn the respect of their elders; they feel adultlike stresses without experiencing the rewards of belonging in the valued settings of adult life.

- **Dominance of Electronic Media.** More than any prior generation in history, young adolescents in America today have become immersed in media. Television and radio, along with personal computers and videocassette recorders, are a dominant presence in the lives of both children and adolescents and a major shaping influence. By mid-adolescence, children have watched about 15,000 hours of television—more time that they have spent with their teachers, their friends, and even their parents.[9] What young people see on television profoundly influences their fears and expectations about the future, their relationships with others, their concept of self and others, and their values.[10]

- **More Pluralism.** The United States has now become one of the leading multiethnic nations in the world. One-third of American adolescents today are of non-European descent and come from a wide array of religious, ethnic, and national backgrounds.[11] In major metropolitan areas, these young people are the majority in the public schools. By the year 2050, close to 50 percent of the entire American population is projected to be African American, American Indian, Asian/Pacific Islander, and Latino/Hispanic.[12] Learning to live peacefully while respecting diversity will be a major task for adults in the twenty-first century.

All adolescents and their families have been affected by these interrelated social transformations, and the pace of change promises only to accelerate in the new century. Consequently, a primary task for American institutions is to find innovative ways to help adolescents adapt to these changes. Such institutional responses are necessary so that individuals of all ages, but especially young people in the midst of profound biological, psychological and social transformation, will be able to build and maintain successful, satisfying lives.

More Education Is Linked to Higher Annual Earnings, 1992

MEAN ANNUAL EARNINGS (IN DOLLARS)

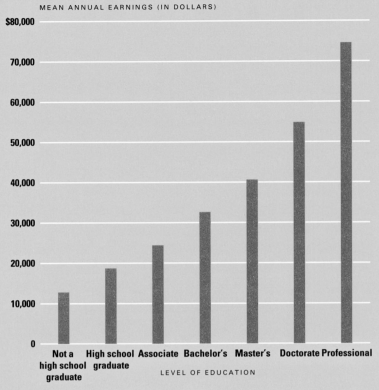

LEVEL OF EDUCATION

Source: "More Education Means Higher Career Earnings," by the U.S. Bureau of the Census, 1994, Washington, DC: Government Printing Office

The Ethnic Composition of Young Adolescents Is Changing, 1995–2050

PERCENTAGE OF YOUTH AGES 10 TO 14

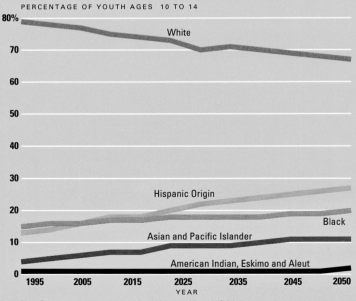

YEAR

Note: Percentages may total more than 100 because Hispanic Origin group overlaps with other ethnic groups.

Source: Population Projections of the United States, by Age, Sex, Race, and Hispanic Origin: 1993 to 2050, by the U.S. Bureau of the Census, 1993, Washington, DC: U.S. Governent Printing Office

Across America, the demands and expectations as well as the risks and opportunities facing adolescents are both more numerous and more complicated than they were even a generation ago. Millions are growing up under conditions that do not meet enduring human needs for optimal development. They are not receiving the careful, nurturing guidance they need from parents and other adults. They are dealing with social pressures to use drugs, including alcohol and cigarettes, and to engage in sex at distressingly early ages. Too many are alienated from school and moving toward dropping out. Many are engaging in antisocial activities and violence.

Although adolescents generally have more autonomy and more money to spend than they used to, they have less real responsibility. Urban neighborhoods once secure are unsafe; even classrooms and hallways can erupt into battlegrounds. With easier access to the weapons and drugs that endanger themselves and others, adolescents have increasing reason to fear each other. Many have not learned how to handle conflict without resorting to violence.

Today younger adolescents are commonly exhibiting many of the very risky behaviors that were once associated with middle and late adolescence. Countless poignant examples exist of troubled, self-destructive, even violent behavior in the ten-to-fourteen-year age group, among rich and poor alike.

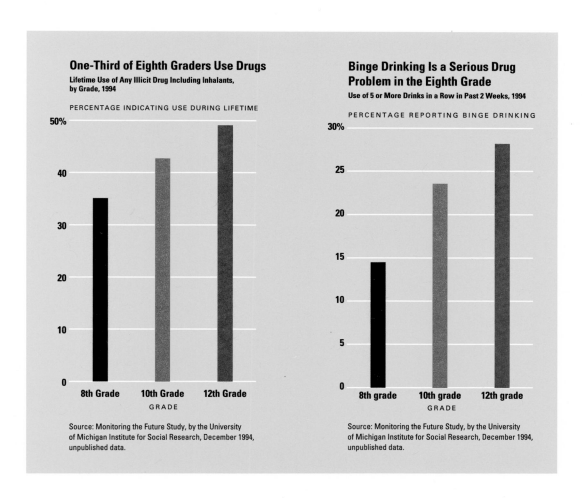

One-Third of Eighth Graders Use Drugs

Lifetime Use of Any Illicit Drug Including Inhalants, by Grade, 1994

PERCENTAGE INDICATING USE DURING LIFETIME

Source: Monitoring the Future Study, by the University of Michigan Institute for Social Research, December 1994, unpublished data.

Binge Drinking Is a Serious Drug Problem in the Eighth Grade

Use of 5 or More Drinks in a Row in Past 2 Weeks, 1994

PERCENTAGE REPORTING BINGE DRINKING

Source: Monitoring the Future Study, by the University of Michigan Institute for Social Research, December 1994, unpublished data.

More Adolescent Males Are Engaging in Sex

PERCENTAGE OF ADOLESCENT MALES WHO HAVE HAD INTERCOURSE

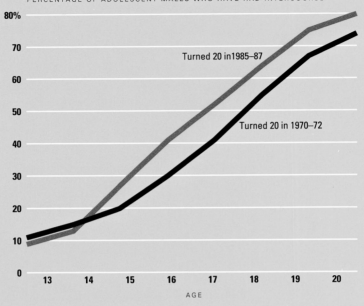

Turned 20 in 1985–87

Turned 20 in 1970–72

AGE

Source: *Sex and America's Teenagers,* by The Alan Guttmacher Institute, 1994, New York:
The Alan Guttmacher Institute. Adapted with permission.

More Adolescent Females Are Engaging in Sex

PERCENTAGE OF ADOLESCENT FEMALES WHO HAVE HAD INTERCOURSE

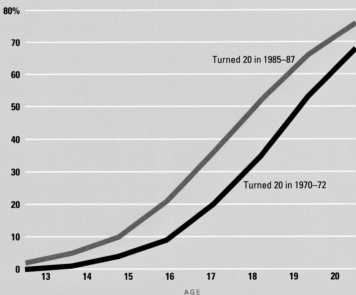

Turned 20 in 1985–87

Turned 20 in 1970–72

AGE

Source: *Sex and America's Teenagers,* by The Alan Guttmacher Institute, 1994,
New York: The Alan Guttmacher Institute. Adapted with permission.

Births to Older Adolescents Remain High, 1972–1992

NUMBER OF BIRTHS, MOTHER 15 TO 19 YEARS OLD

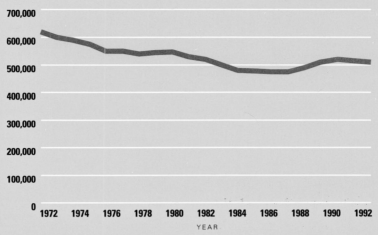

Source: Tabulations by American Demographics, Inc., 1995, based on National Center for Health Statistics unpublished data. Adapted with permission.

Births to Young Adolescents Are Rising, 1972–1992

NUMBER OF BIRTHS, MOTHER YOUNGER THAN 15 YEARS OLD

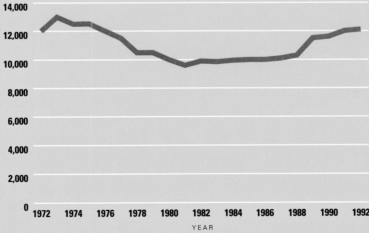

Source: Tabulations by American Demographics, Inc., 1995, based on National Center for Health Statistics unpublished data. Adapted with permission.

- **Earlier Experimentation with Drugs.** A troubling number of young adolescents are smoking cigarettes and drinking alcohol. They perceive little or no risk to using these addictive substances, which are gateways to the use of illicit drugs (including marijuana, LSD and other hallucinogens, inhalants, stimulants, barbiturates, cocaine, and crack). Fully one-third of eighth graders reported using an illicit drug in 1994.[13]

- **Earlier Sexual Activity.** Rates of sexual initiation are increasing among younger girls and boys.[14] Many American teenagers are startlingly ignorant of the most elementary facts of the human body and human sexuality, despite their wholesale exposure to sex in the mass media, the availability of sexually related materials, and efforts to provide sexuality education in the schools. Among teenagers in the United States, pregnancy rates are higher than in any other industrialized nation.[15] In 1990, adolescents gave birth to 12 percent of all newborns. Four percent were to those under age eighteen, and 8 percent were to eighteen- and nineteen-year-olds.[16]

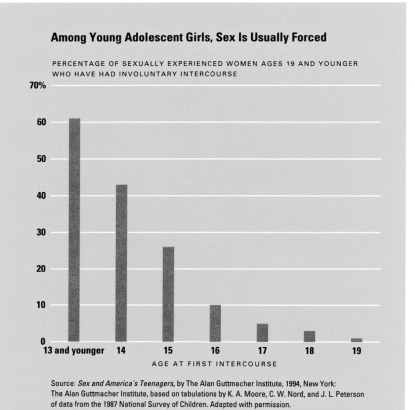

Among Young Adolescent Girls, Sex Is Usually Forced

PERCENTAGE OF SEXUALLY EXPERIENCED WOMEN AGES 19 AND YOUNGER WHO HAVE HAD INVOLUNTARY INTERCOURSE

AGE AT FIRST INTERCOURSE

Source: *Sex and America's Teenagers,* by The Alan Guttmacher Institute, 1994, New York: The Alan Guttmacher Institute, based on tabulations by K. A. Moore, C. W. Nord, and J. L. Peterson of data from the 1987 National Survey of Children. Adapted with permission.

- **Inadequate Learning.** In the past two decades, achievement levels and rates of high school graduation have remained virtually stagnant.[17] The performance of American students is lower than that of same-aged students in both Asia and Europe. Such performance is too low to support increasing living standards in a high-technology, information-based society.

- **More health-damaging behavior.** As the communicable diseases of childhood have been controlled by biomedical research and public health advances, new behavior-based morbidities of adolescence have come to the fore.[18] Suicide and gun-related homicides are at record-high levels.[19] Injury, homicide, and suicide taken together account for most adolescent deaths.[20]

By age eighteen, about a quarter of all adolescents have engaged in behavior that is harmful or dangerous to themselves or others. Another quarter are deemed at moderate risk for such behavior. On average, about half of all American adolescents—an estimated 14 million girls and boys—are at high or moderate risk of impairing their life chances through engaging in problem behaviors.[21] In distressed communities, the proportion of adolescents at very high risk for poor outcomes is even larger.

The Science and Mathematics Achievement of American 13-Year-Olds Is a Serious Concern

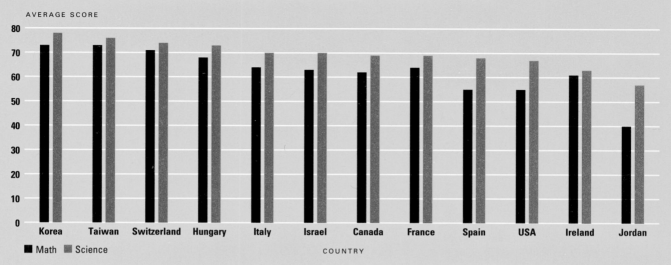

AVERAGE SCORE

■ Math ■ Science

COUNTRY

Source: *Learning Math* and *Learning Science,* by A. E. Lapointe, N. A. Mead, and J. M. Askew, 1992, Princeton, NJ: Educational Testing Service. Adapted with permission.

Percentage of Adolescents Ages 10 to 14 Living Below the Poverty Line, 1993

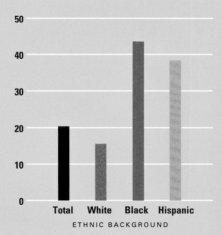

ETHNIC BACKGROUND

Source: Current Population Survey, by the U.S. Bureau of the Census, March 1994, unpublished data.

Living in Distressed Neighborhoods

PERCENTAGE OF YOUTHS YOUNGER THAN AGE 18

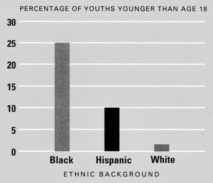

ETHNIC BACKGROUND

Note: A distressed neighborhood is defined by high levels (at least one standard deviation above the mean) of: (1) poverty; (2) female-headed families; (3) high school dropouts; (4) unemployment; and (5) reliance on welfare.

Source: *Kids Count Data Book 1994: State Profiles of Child Well-Being,* by the Annie E. Casey Foundation, 1994, Baltimore, MD: Annie E. Casey Foundation. Adapted with permission.

Leading Causes of Death in Adolescents by Age, 1992

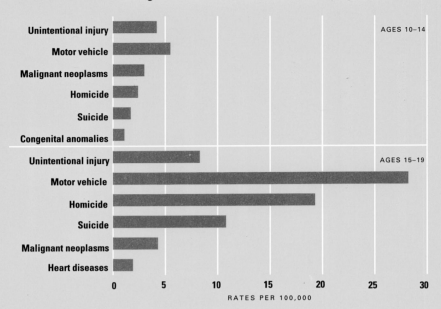

AGES 10–14

- Unintentional injury
- Motor vehicle
- Malignant neoplasms
- Homicide
- Suicide
- Congenital anomalies

AGES 15–19

- Unintentional injury
- Motor vehicle
- Homicide
- Suicide
- Malignant neoplasms
- Heart diseases

RATES PER 100,000

Note: A recent addition to the leading causes of death for adolescents aged 15–19 is infection with the human immunodeficiency virus (HIV). HIV infection was the tenth leading cause of death for this age group, at a rate of 0.3 per 100,000.

Source: The National Center for Health Statistics, 1994, unpublished data.

The Rate of Suicide Is Rising Among White and Black Adolescents, 1980–1992

PERCENTAGE CHANGE, 1980 TO 1992

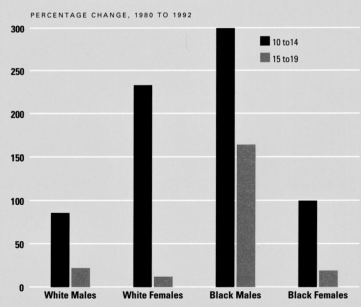

■ 10 to14
■ 15 to19

White Males   White Females   Black Males   Black Females

Source: "Suicide among Children, Adolescents, and Young Adults—United States, 1980–1992," April 21, 1995, *Morbidity and Mortality Weekly Report, 44,* (15).

Firearm Deaths of 10- to 14-Year-Olds, 1980–1992

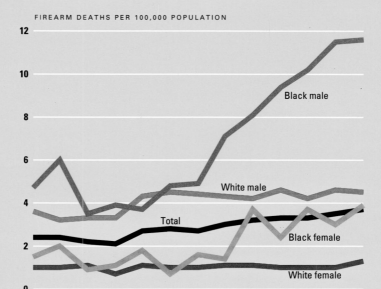

FIREARM DEATHS PER 100,000 POPULATION

Black male

White male

Total

Black female

White female

YEARS

Source: "Firearm Mortality among Children, Youth, and Young Adults 1–34 Years of Age, Trends
and Current Status: United States, 1979–88," by L. Fingerhut, J. C. Kleinman, E. Godfrey,
and H. Rosenberg, 1991, *Monthly Vital Statistics Report, 39*, (11); and National Center for Health
Statistics, data from the National Vital Statistics program, 1994, unpublished data.

Firearm Deaths of 15- to 19-Year-Olds, 1980 to 1992

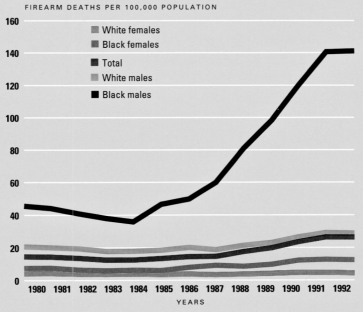

FIREARM DEATHS PER 100,000 POPULATION

White females
Black females
Total
White males
Black males

YEARS

Source: "Firearm Mortality among Children, Youth, and Young Adults 1–34 Years of Age,
Trends and Current Status: United States, 1979–88,"by L. Fingerhut, J. C. Kleinman, E. Godfrey ,
and H. Rosenberg, 1991, Monthly Vital Statistics Report, 39, (11): and National Center for Health Statistics,
data from the National Vital Statistics program, 1994, unputlished data.

Overcoming The Odds

Even adolescents at risk of developing serious learning or behavior problems can beat the odds and increase their chances to lead successful adult lives. A three-decade, longitudinal study of all children born on the island of Kaua'i, Hawai'i, in 1955 offers us some clues about what makes for resiliency under adversity and how the design of effective prevention strategies can be informed by naturally occurring interventions.

One-third of Kaua'i's Asian Pacific American children were designated as "high risk" because they were born into chronic poverty, had experienced perinatal stress, and lived in families plagued by conflict, divorce, alcoholism, or mental disorders. By age eighteen, two-thirds of this high-risk group did experience problems, including delinquency, mental health problems, or teenage pregnancy. The remaining children were described by researchers Emmy Werner and Ruth S. Smith as "vulnerable, but resilient," and they emerged as competent young adults who were gainfully employed, involved in stable relationships with spouses or partners, and active in their communities. None developed problems during childhood or adolescence.

Three clusters of protective factors distinguished this "resilient" group from the other high-risk individuals who did develop problems by adolescence: (1) temperamental characteristics and engaging social skills, which involve family members and others, and at least average intelligence; (2) strong attachments with parents or parental substitutes, including grandparents and siblings; and (3) a broad community support system such as a church, youth group, or school that offered stable support and consistent guidance, with the hope that they could expect a good future. In this and more than 250 studies of children growing up in adverse circumstances—war, poverty, dysfunctional families—results present a consistent picture that these common factors enable young people to beat the odds.

Even for the Kaua'i adolescents with problems, the vast majority became successful adults by their early thirties. Their experiences with supportive people and structured lives—such as joining the military or a church group, having close and stable relationships with caring mates or spouses, and obtaining postsecondary education —provided opportunities to turn their lives around. These results are consistent with those from other communities where taking on adult roles as workers, parents, and spouses can overturn adolescent deviance. In all cases, the commitment of nurturing, competent adults to a young person is crucial. For some, the adults were parents, but for others, they were concerned teachers, coaches, youth workers, or relatives.

Werner emphasized the importance of naturally occurring informal support networks in shaping the life trajectories of adolescents who overcome great odds. Where such support networks do not exist as they did on Kaua'i, "a continuum of care and caring by professionals as well as volunteers" is required. The children of Kaua'i, who are now adults approaching middle age, and children in similar studies throughout the world offer compelling testimony about what can make a difference in lives threatened by conditions of economic and personal adversity.

SOURCES

Werner, E. E., & Smith, R. S. (1992). *Overcoming the odds: High-risk children from birth to adulthood.* Ithaca, NY: Cornell University Press.

Werner, E. E., & Smith, R. S. (1983). *Vulnerable but invincible: A study of resilient children.* New York: McGraw-Hill.

Werner, E. E., Bierman, J. M., & French, F. E. (1971). *The children of Kauai: A longitudinal study from the prenatal period to age ten.* Honolulu: University of Hawai'i Press.

Many low-income neighborhoods lack jobs that generate adequate family incomes, thus concentrating poverty in a way that pervades the community.[22] There, young people are rarely exposed to role models who can raise their expectations about stable jobs and family life. Few adults are available for sustained attention, guidance, and supervision. Areas of concentrated poverty have high crime rates and dangerous streets. Young adolescents from these areas often are tempted to get involved with illicit drugs, not only as users but also as sellers. They spend a lot of time alone, often watching television with all its vivid violence and putative badges of adulthood and hanging out on street corners where real violence threatens or with antisocial peer groups. They may be engaged in sexual activity earlier than their parents were, even as they disengage from school.

Not all troubled adolescents are disadvantaged, and not all disadvantaged adolescents are troubled. But adolescents from economically disadvantaged backgrounds are often at higher risk than their more privileged counterparts of reaching adulthood ill equipped for work, family life, and full participation in our democratic society. They are more apt to be indifferent to their health and cynical about future opportunities that could motivate them to adopt health-enhancing behavior.[23] They are more likely to bear children in adolescence—indeed, 87 percent of teen mothers are poor or near poor.[24] Yet, even high-risk behavior need not be the case, as shown by a recent decline in smoking reported by African American adolescents.[25] As we shall see, there is much that can usefully be done for young people even in circumstances of deep adversity.

TURNING NEW RISKS TO NEW OPPORTUNITIES

Although the profound changes of adolescence create vulnerability, they also provide a unique window of opportunity. Adolescents initially explore new behavior patterns and possibilities tentatively. That is why, before damaging patterns are firmly established, adults have a major opportunity to shape interventions to prevent later casualties and promote more successful outcomes.

Adolescence represents the last phase of the life course during which society has reasonably ready access to the entire population, so the potential for constructive influence is great. With the supportive guidance of pivotal institutions, namely the family, schools, community and health-care organizations, and media, adolescents can be helped to form healthier, problem-solving lifestyles and thereby increase their odds of successfully meeting the challenges of adult life in a transformed world.

■ ■ ■ ■ ■ ■ ■ ■

Further Reading

Commission on Behavioral and Social Sciences and Education, National Research Council. (1993). *Losing generations: Adolescents in high-risk settings.* Washington, DC: National Academy Press.

Dryfoos, J. G. (1990). *Adolescents at risk: Prevalence and prevention.* New York: Oxford University Press.

Hawley, W. D., & Jackson, A. W. (Eds.). (1995). *Toward a common destiny: Improving race and ethnic relations in America.* San Francisco: Jossey-Bass.

Reducing Risks, Enhancing Opportunities: Essential Requirements for Healthy Development

Although new social circumstances have vastly altered the landscape for adolescent development, all adolescents continue to have fundamental human requirements that must be met if they are to grow up into healthy, constructive adults. All run the risk of diminished lives if these requirements are not met.

To make a successful transition to adulthood, adolescents must still have the kind of help and support that was once commonly available within the network of family and kin but now is eroded. They must have sustained, caring relationships with adults; receive guidance in facing serious challenges; become a valued member of a constructive peer group; feel a sense of worth as a person; become socially competent; know how to use the support systems available to them; achieve a reliable basis for making informed choices; find constructive expression of the curiosity and exploration that strongly characterize their age; believe in a promising future with real opportunities; and find ways of being useful to others.

Meeting these requirements has been basic for survival into adulthood for millennia. But in a democratic society that places an increasingly high premium on competence in many domains, adolescents now face an even stiffer set of challenges. They must learn the elements of responsible citizenship; master social skills, including the ability to manage conflict peacefully; become ethical persons; respect diversity in our pluralistic society; and cultivate inquiring and problem-solving habits of mind. Further, to compete for good jobs in a rapidly changing workplace, young people must not only acquire the technical and analytical capabilities to participate in a worldwide economy, they must also have motivation for lifelong learning and for adaptability throughout the life span. Indeed, an important part of preparation for adulthood today is preparation for change itself.

Many of the adolescents who have serious problems lack critical social supports and are at risk of not meeting the challenges of the twenty-first century. Serious adolescent problems, such as delinquency, substance abuse, adolescent pregnancy, and school failure, are strongly associated with family discord or violence, poor communication, lack of parental monitoring, and inconsistent discipline.[1] They are typically associated with parents who are either highly authoritarian or very permissive in their child-rearing practices.

One of the important insights to emerge from scientific inquiry into adolescence in the past two decades is that problem behaviors tend to cluster in the same individual and reinforce one another.[2] Crime, school dropout, teenage childbearing, and drug abuse typically are considered separately, but in the real world they occur together. Those who drink and smoke in early adolescence are thus more likely to initiate sex earlier than their peers; those who engage in these behavior patterns often have a history of difficulties in school. When young people have a low commitment to school and education, and when teachers or parents have low expectations of the children's performance, trouble lurks. Once educational failure occurs, then other adverse events begin to take hold.

Just as health-compromising behaviors cluster, health-enhancing behaviors of young adolescents also tend to be linked.[3] These observations suggest that families, schools, and other social institutions have a unique opportunity to foster healthy lifestyles during early adolescence by addressing the common roots of both positive and negative behavioral clusters. Such an approach to adolescent development is *generic*, to distinguish it from a *categorical* or targeted approach that focuses on a specific or single problem. Generic approaches emphasize the positive possibilities inherent in the adolescent transition: possibilities for educating and motivating adolescents in the pursuit of healthy lifestyles;[4] for fostering interpersonal and decision-making skills to help them choose alternatives to very risky behavior;[5] and for providing them with ways to build constructive lives.

Generic interventions address some of the underlying or predisposing factors that increase the likelihood that an adolescent will engage in high-risk or problem behaviors. These factors include low self-esteem, underdeveloped interpersonal and decision-making skills, lack of interest in education, inadequate information regarding health matters, low perception of opportunities, the absence of dependable and close human relationships, and meager incentives for delaying short-term gratification.

Generic approaches seek to meet the fundamental developmental needs of adolescents and promote a cluster of healthy behaviors that are likely to emerge when these needs are met. Generic approaches are especially useful for the population of young people who are at moderate risk of negative outcomes and who, therefore, can readily go either way: toward additional problem behavior or toward healthy adolescent development.

There is a complementary relationship between generic approaches that tackle these underlying factors and targeted approaches that deal with specific problems. For instance, a generic approach can help a shaky adolescent earn self-respect, find a place in a valued and constructive group, and make durable friendships, all of which enhance the individual's resistance to

New Jersey Offers Comprehensive Services for Youth

Trouble for many young adolescents comes in multiple doses. A young person may have parents who face unemployment and housing problems or may have a father or mother who is an alcoholic or drug abuser. The young person may be performing poorly at school, may lack adequate medical or dental care, and may know no reliable adult to whom to turn to for advice.

Human service agencies that could help these young people may themselves be geographically dispersed, unattractively labeled or socially unacceptable to adolescents, and not linked to one another. The agencies may rely heavily on informal referrals, with no systematic way of accepting students from the school system. Furthermore, if the agencies do not provide family counseling, they may be unable or unwilling to address problems in family relationships. One promising state-based model to provide needed help for adolescents is New Jersey's School- Based Youth Services Program, which brings together existing services for adolescents under one roof, most often at the school. State officials have found that schools offer the most effective sites for reaching and assisting large numbers of adolescents on a regular basis.

Led by then-Governor Thomas Kean, the New Jersey Department of Human Resources initiated the School-Based Youth Services Program in 1988 as a way of connecting the state's education, health, and human services, and creating "one-stop service centers" for adolescents and their families. By changing the traditional institutional arrangements of the state's agencies from a targeted approach to one that supports the overall well-being of the state's teenagers by providing comprehensive services, this program has encouraged teenagers to complete their education, obtain the skills they need for employment or for additional education, and lead healthy, productive lives.

Today the program operates in thirty-seven sites in or near schools in urban, rural, and suburban communities. Sites are open during and after school, on weekends, and all summer long. They offer a core set of services, all of which require parental consent. Centers offer adolescents basic services: primary and preventive health services; referrals to health and social services; individual and family counseling; crisis intervention; drug and alcohol abuse counseling; employment counseling, training, and placement; summer and part-time job development; and recreation. Beyond this core of services, the state encourages centers to provide classroom-based health education; arts, cooking, and sports activities; transportation; family planning examinations and referrals; parenting skills instruction; violence prevention programs; child care; outreach to adolescents who have left school; or twenty-four-hour hotlines. Mental health services are the most frequently used service across the state, followed by other health, employment, education, and substance abuse services.

In 1991, about one of every three New Jersey teenagers—more than 19,000 students—participated in this state-sponsored program. A recent survey revealed that more than half of the students receiving services are African American and nearly a quarter are Hispanic. More than half of the adolescents are considered at risk for dropping out of school. Girls and boys use the service about equally, and they are most likely to be ninth and tenth graders.

Although evaluative data are not yet extensive, programs like New Jersey's appear to be efficient, cost-effective ways to connect adolescents and their families to critical services. Administratively, the state requires that each host community provide at least 25 percent of the program costs through direct financial contribution or in-kind services, facilities, or materials. Each site costs the state approximately

$230,000 annually, or about $200 per student served. Stable funding is a strong factor in convincing community organizations and schools that they should work together on the program.

At Plainfield High School, in response to the incidence of teenage parenthood, the Plainfield School-Based Youth Services Program developed and implemented the Plainfield Teen Parent Program in collaboration with the Parent Linking Project of the New Jersey Chapter, National Committee for Prevention of Child Abuse, AT&T, Community Coordinated Child Care of Union County, and the Plainfield Health Center. The program provides a comprehensive array of services to mothers and their babies, including school-based child care, parent education classes, mentoring, tutoring, parent support groups for both pregnant and parenting teens, life skills training, job skills training, health care, including prenatal, well-baby, and adolescent health care, and information and referral to other social service agencies. Services are also provided to young fathers, grandparents, and guardians. All students who have children in the Plainfield Infant Toddler Center are required to enroll in a parenting class that teaches the student-parents activities to enhance their child's development and to strengthen the parent-child relationship. Parent support groups provide an opportunity for students to talk about what it is like to raise children as they struggle for their own independence. Students are encouraged to share their ideas and experiences, to see their similarities and differences, and to help each other solve problems and work through tough times.

An evaluation of the project found that 84 percent of program mothers graduated from high school, compared to 41 percent of the control mothers. Two years after their first births, 11 percent of program mothers had a second birth, compared to 33 percent of the control mothers. Program mothers were more likely than comparison mothers to report having a regular source of medical care for their children. Stress associated with parenting decreased significantly among program mothers, while general self-esteem rose. Students and faculty at Plainfield High School generally supported the presence of a child-care center on the school grounds and felt that it made a difference in making it possible for some girls to graduate. This program was developed by and includes representatives from all segments of the community and private and public sectors.

drugs, weapons, or early sexual activity. At the same time, it is important for adolescents to acquire accurate information about each of these major risks and to develop specific skills in avoiding them. In this way, the generic and targeted approaches are mutually supportive.

SOCIAL SUPPORTS TO ADOLESCENTS AND FAMILIES

At the heart of a generic approach to adolescent development is the restoration and strengthening of social supports that once were available to young adolescents within their families and communities. A working group on social support networks, established by the Carnegie Council on Adolescent Development and chaired by Richard Price of the University of Michigan, examined the potential of schools and youth organizations to offer young adolescents the practical services and material benefits that promote healthy development; the feedback that raises self-esteem and strengthens identity; and the affection, caring, and nurture they need. Carefully reviewing dozens of such programs across a variety of settings, the working group noted the following critical ingredients of effective or promising approaches:[6]

- *They tend to respond to more than one serious problem or risk factor.* They recognize that adolescent problems occur in clusters.

- *They plan interventions in ways that can make a difference before damaging patterns are firmly established.* They take developmental information into account—for instance, they take note of the point at which high-risk behavior is likely to begin in offering guidance to the young to diminish the risks.

- *They create incentives that adolescents are likely to perceive as relevant to their own lives.* For example, they open up social roles that are respected and provide the opportunity to learn new skills. They tend to provide some combination of knowledge and skill that can help young people earn respect.

- *They are broad enough in scope and flexible enough in mode of operation to adapt to a considerable range of needs.*

SUPPORT STRATEGIES FOR CREATING MEANINGFUL SOCIAL ROLES

One of the problems adolescents have is that they often do not perceive what their place is in society or what they are being prepared for.[7] They wonder how they can earn appreciation and approval. Particular support strategies have arisen to foster meaningful social roles for them during early adolescence. These strategies include adult mentoring, peer tutoring, and service to others in the community. Successful efforts to help prepare young people for adult social roles share the following characteristics:[8]

- *They foster active participation by adolescents.* They provide opportunities for direct involvement, high initiative, and leadership. For example, they may arrange for rotation of leadership in group activities and construct opportunities for adolescents to give as well as to receive.

- *They foster relationships among several elements of the social support system.* For example, there are programs aimed at preventing school failure that actively engage both teachers and parents, helping each to understand the adolescent better and to work together in supporting efforts to improve the students' educational performance.

- *They provide considerable continuity over time.* They are arranged to provide dependable, trusting relationships for one year or longer, providing incentives and guidance for adolescents to pursue a constructive course with respect to their health and education.

- *They promote activities that fit well in sponsoring organizations.* They try to build upon organizational readiness for change.

ADULT MENTORING

A crucial need of adolescents is for an enduring, stable, supportive bond with a caring adult. For this reason, another aspect of social support that has captured great interest in recent years, especially for its benefits in communities with very low incomes, is adult mentoring.[9] A variety of innovative efforts have explored ways to construct such dependable one-to-one relations over an extended period of time.

Mentoring can be a powerful way to provide adult involvement with adolescents who are largely isolated from the world of adults. It can help adolescents prepare for social roles that earn respect and encourage them to persist in education. Elder citizens can contribute substantially as mentors to adolescents, bringing new meaning to their own lives while helping the younger generation grow up. On the basis of this trusting and stimulating experience, other relationships may be built in the future. However, the mentor's task is not easy. He or she is expected to provide sustained support, guidance, and concrete assistance as the adolescent goes through a difficult time, enters a new situation, or takes on new tasks. It is also important that a mentoring program be integrated with other resources in the community. Particularly for high-risk youth, where problems tend to cluster, the connection with education, health, and social services is necessary.

PEER-MEDIATED PROGRAMS THAT PROMOTE HEALTH AND EDUCATION

Peer relations in adolescence are powerful influences, for better or worse. Within the group, there can be opportunities to become a person worthy of respect, with a distinctive contribution to make. Programs led by peers can be valuable in giving young adolescents the ongoing, sympathetic attention they need to cope with risk factors. The credibility of peers during adolescence can help some young people who would otherwise be very hard to reach. Both education- and health-oriented interventions can function well with peer leadership, if teachers or other professional adults provide proper training and supervision. Indeed, continuing guidance of peer tutors and counselors by mature, qualified adults is important.

Peer-led programs on smoking, for example, show they can substantially reduce the onset of smoking in early adolescence.[10] In these programs, older peer leaders who themselves have successfully resisted the lure of addictive substances can serve as models for young ones only now on the verge. Peer leaders can be effective in teaching younger adolescents social skills to resist pressures to use drugs or engage in premature sex and can help them identify and practice health-enhancing behaviors.

Abundant evidence also exists of the value of one-to-one tutoring as an effective teaching method. With a trained tutor, 98 percent of students do better in school than they otherwise would.[11] This is true not only when the tutoring is conducted by teachers or professional tutors; it also works well when the tutor is a suitably prepared student, especially one who is older. Students in elementary and secondary school can benefit from tutoring by older peers in difficult subjects such as mathematics.

As with peer counseling, there is considerable evidence that tutoring benefits the young tutors.[12] When these programs are firmly established, teachers also benefit.[13] The classroom climate is likely to improve. Since fewer students are feeling left out or seriously alienated, a more cooperative atmosphere conducive to learning tends to emerge. A well-functioning program of students serving as auxiliary teachers allows teachers to use their professional skills more fully than they could otherwise.

If adolescents are to solve problems of human relations, develop healthy lifestyles, access social systems, cultivate intellectual curiosity, and meet the demands of the workplace, they must learn basic life skills. By and large, these are practical skills that help in coping with day-to-day living. In favorable circumstances, adolescents acquire these critical adaptive skills in the family, in friendship groups, in the neighborhood, and in school. To the extent that families and neighborhood resources are unable to fulfill these requirements, however, specially designed interventions may be crucial.

In considering ways to prevent damaging outcomes in education and health during adolescence, the Carnegie Council on Adolescent Development has given in-depth scrutiny to the role of specific training in such "life skills," especially in early adolescence, when young people are making fateful decisions that involve education, drugs, weapons, and how they use their bodies.[14] Such training offered at this decisive time can capitalize on young adolescents' emerging cognitive capabilities—marked by a change from the concrete thinking of childhood to the capacity for higher-order thinking—to develop the social skills and competence needed for success in the mainstream.

Life skills training should become a vital part of education in all relevant institutions, including most especially the family, schools, and community-based organizations, so that adolescents learn to make informed, deliberate, and constructive decisions. Such decision making requires one to stop and think, obtain information and assess it, formulate or consider options, try new behavior, and get feedback. Linked to a curriculum in the life sciences in middle grade and junior high schools, for example, life skills training could answer many questions that adolescents have about their bodies and how to use them responsibly.

One such life skill that adolescents often lack and that can be taught is the ability to pursue constructive relations with others. Adolescents who are vulnerable because they have been isolated and lonely, depressed, angry, and lacking in interpersonal skills can be helped through life skills training to form solid friendships, learn from experience, and participate in cooperative groups. Another useful skill is assertiveness. An aspect of assertiveness is knowing how to resist pressure or intimidation to use drugs or weapons or have sex—without disrupting valued relationships or isolating oneself. Yet another aspect is nonviolent conflict resolution—the ability to achieve personal and social goals in ways that make use of the many nonviolent opportunities that exist in the society.

> I think that being a kid is the most important stage of your life. It's a time when you start to develop a personality. It's when you start to learn about who you are, and what you want to do with yourself. And it's a time when you develop trust. It's a time when you learn how to be a person in society.
>
> Unfortunately a lot of kids don't have that. If you don't grow up learning how to be a productive person, then you're going to have a problem once you grow up.
>
> **SARAH ROSEN, 16**

Mentors Rewrite the Future of Youth

A downward trajectory is not inevitable for youth living in neighborhoods of concentrated poverty. Young people from extremely disadvantaged situations can rewrite their futures with the help of a caring adult mentor from the community if the mentoring takes place in combination with a multiyear mix of educational, developmental, and cultural activities and with service to others in the community. The Quantum Opportunities Program (QOP), a four-year, year-round youth development program, funded by The Ford Foundation, has shown that intervening during the high school years, beginning during the freshman year (age thirteen), can more than marginally improve the prospects for African American adolescents in poverty. The program, initiated during the 1989–1990 school year, was designed to test the ability of community-based organizations to foster academic and social competencies among high school students from families receiving public assistance.

Participants were selected at random from high schools in five sites—Philadelphia, Oklahoma City, Saginaw, Milwaukee, and San Antonio. Students were eligible for the program if they were entering the ninth grade, attending a public high school in a neighborhood with high rates of poverty, a member of a minority group, and from a family receiving public assistance. Each group of twenty-five students at the five sites was matched with a paid mentor who stayed with the group for the four years of high school, including summers. Extremely committed to their students, mentors provided what children need most—an adult who cares about them and who sticks with them over the long term no matter what. Each day for four years, mentors provided sustained support, guidance, and concrete assistance to their students, all of whom were growing up in poverty.

The program required students to participate in (1) academic-related activities outside school hours, including reading, writing, math, science, and social studies, peer tutoring, and computer skills training; (2) community service projects, including tutoring elementary school students, cleaning up the neighborhood, and volunteering in hospitals, nursing homes, and libraries; and (3) cultural enrichment and personal development activities, including life skills training, college and job planning, attending plays and concerts, visiting museums, and reading and discussing the great books. Community service activities connected the students to their communities and helped them develop many of the skills needed for work—reliability, following through on tasks, and working cooperatively. Through personal development activities, students learned how to set goals, manage their time, and choose behavior appropriate for varying situations. They learned the life skills needed in the home, at work, and in the marketplace. Consequently, the program encouraged students to develop meaningful relationship with their mentors, form strong ties to their peers because of the family-like environment provided by the program, and strengthen their ties to their neighborhoods through service.

In exchange for their commitment to the program, students were offered financial incentives that encouraged participation, completion, and long-range planning. A stipend of $1.33 was given to students for each hour they participated in these activities. For every 100 hours of education, service, or development activities in a cycle, students received a completion bonus payment of $100. The accrued amount with interest became available to the student for college, job training, technical training, or other approved education upon graduation from high school. The average cost per participant was $10,600 for the four years, which is one-half the cost of a year in prison.

Brandeis University faculty conducted an evaluation of the program using a random-assignment control-group design to assess effects while students were in the program and after they graduated. The results are encouraging. The fall 1993 follow-up evaluation of participants and controls in three sites (Philadel-phia, Saginaw, and Oklahoma City) shows the effec-tiveness of an intensive effort that offers an array of coordinated services, coupled with a continuing relationship with a peer group and a caring adult. Sixty-three percent of program participants gradu-ated from high school, and 42 percent are currently enrolled in college, versus 42 percent and 16 per-cent, respectively, of the controls. Program partici-pants bore fewer children than controls (24 percent compared to 38 percent of control group members). In addition, participants were half as likely to receive food stamps or welfare and average fewer arrests than controls (19 percent compared to 23 percent). QOP members are significantly more likely to be in-volved in community service, to be hopeful about their future, and to consider their life a success than are control group members.

To students like Jacqueline Jones, participation in the program has made a difference. She said it has given her a sense of "respect, trust, friendship, and, most important, love. It has been a vital part of my life and education. It helped to enhance my knowledge and understanding of the world I live in. . . . I got in-volved in the community by doing community ser-vices, and helping others as the QOP program had helped me."

As part of The Ford Foundation's continuing support, the program will be tested further in five additional sites that include approximately 700 participants. A key ingredient of this program is the sustained in-volvement of community organizations and residents. Given the interest in empowering local communities, this program offers a working model that has the po-tential to overcome the intergenerational transmis-sion of poverty and its negative outcomes.

SOURCE

Hahn, A., Leavitt, T., & Aaron, P. (1994). *Evaluation of the quantum opportunities program (QOP). Did the program work?* Waltham, MA: Brandeis University.

Substance Abuse Prevention and Life Skills Training

Training in life skills is an essential part of a comprehensive approach to prevent adolescents from engaging in health-compromising behaviors. Through life skills, young adolescents can learn to enhance their competence to resist social influences that result in high-risk behaviors. This prevention strategy is designed to help young people, particularly in middle or junior high school, develop basic personal and social skills and an increased sense of control by teaching them to apply and practice skills that are relevant to the social situations that adolescents confront. The program objectives of life skills training are to:

■ Provide students with the necessary skills to resist social pressures to smoke cigarettes, drink alcohol excessively, or use marijuana;

■ Decrease students' susceptibility to social pressures to use tobacco, alcohol, and other drugs by helping them develop greater autonomy, self-esteem, and confidence;

■ Teach students to resist the influence of advertising that promotes addictive substances;

■ Enable students to cope effectively with anxiety, particularly anxiety induced by social situations;

■ Increase awareness of the negative consequences of substance use, particularly the more immediate physical and social consequences;

■ Correct normative expectations concerning substance use by providing them with accurate information concerning the actual prevalence rates of tobacco, alcohol misuse, and marijuana use.

In evaluating the long-term efficacy of a school-based approach to drug abuse prevention, Gilbert Botvin and his colleagues found significant reductions in both drug and polydrug use (tobacco, alcohol, marijuana) in a random sample of twelfth-grade students who had received a life skills intervention while in the seventh grade. The intervention consisted of fifteen classes taught in seventh grade, ten booster sessions in eighth grade, and five booster sessions in ninth grade. The booster sessions were designed to review and reinforce the material covered during the first year of intervention.

The main focus of the intervention was on imparting information and skills for resisting social influences to use drugs and generic personal and social skills for increasing overall competence and promoting the development of characteristics associated with decreased risk of using drugs. In contrast to other prevention programs, only minimal information concerning the long-term health consequences of drug use was provided. Information relevant to adolescents in their daily lives was taught, including the immediate negative consequences of drug use, the decreasing social acceptability of use, and the actual prevalence rates among adults and adolescents.

Findings from this six-year follow-up study suggest that drug abuse prevention programs conducted during junior high school can produce significant and sustained reductions in tobacco, alcohol, and marijuana use if they teach a combination of social resistance skills (including general life skills), are properly implemented, and are followed by at least two years of booster sessions.

SOURCES

Botvin, G.J., Baker, E., Dusenbury, L., Botvin, E.M., & Diaz, T. (1995). Long-term follow-up results of a randomized drug abuse prevention trial in a white middle-class population. *Journal of the American Medical Association, 273,* 1106–1112.

Hamburg, B.A. (1990). *Life skills training: Preventive interventions for young adolescents.* Washington, DC: Carnegie Council on Adolescent Development.

Recent research has shown that life skills training can help prevent adolescent problem behavior.[15] When tasks are clarified and appropriate skills provided, negative attitudes can be changed and adolescent motivation strengthened to tackle life's problems. To be successful, however, life skills must become a part of daily life and must be reinforced. Increasingly, training in life skills is being oriented toward disadvantaged youths in impoverished social environments, to good effect.[16]

COMPREHENSIVE SOLUTIONS FOR INTERRELATED PROBLEMS

All these approaches—strengthening social support networks, establishing meaningful social roles for adolescents, creating adult mentoring opportunities, fostering peer-mediated programs, and developing life skills training—are generic in character. They have the potential to prevent a wide range of problems in adolescent health and education.

The enduring significance of a comprehensive approach is that it responds directly to the basic requirements of adolescents as they begin to move toward adulthood. Adults and institutions can address these aspirations, meeting adolescents halfway in seeking fulfillment. The chapters that follow in Part II review the most promising approaches available by which tomorrow's institutions can create such generic interventions, building on today's strengths to offer young adolescents a decent chance in life.

■ ■ ■ ■ ■ ■ ■ ■

Further Reading

Dryfoos, J. G. (1994). *Full-service schools: A revolution in health and social services for children, youth, and families*. San Francisco: Jossey-Bass.

Hamburg, B. A. (1990). *Life skills training: Preventive interventions for young adolescents*. Washington, DC: Carnegie Council on Adolescent Development.

Hamburg, D. A. (1992). *Today's children: Creating a future for a generation in crisis*. New York: Times Books.

Price, R. H., Cioci, M., Penner, W., & Trautlein, B. (1990). *School and community support programs that enhance adolescent health and education*. Washington, DC: Carnegie Council on Adolescent Development.

PART II

Preparing Adolescents for a New Century

WHAT'S COOKING IN NATURE'S KITCHEN

The World
½ cup good times
½ cup bad
equal shares work, play
¼ cup tithing
pinch of death
1 cup love

Simmer violence, prejudice, hate.
Melt into loving hearts.

Summer—Stir the world
Fall—Bake and cool
Winter—Ice with hearts
Enjoy in Spring

MICHELLE MONIZ, 13

Reengaging Families with Their Adolescent Children

Being a parent of an adolescent in today's America is a formidable responsibility. Within our lifetime, dramatic changes have occurred in the structure of American families and of the workplace. There are many more single or divorced parents and more two-worker families than existed a generation ago. Many parents must take two jobs to make ends meet. These changes have decreased the time parents have available for supervising their children and for instilling values. With all the dislocations in the global economy, parents are uncertain about their children's future. On a more immediate level, both adolescents and their parents report that life is more difficult and neighborhoods more dangerous than in the past.[1]

Many parents see their teenagers drifting into an amorphous, risky peer milieu popularly termed "the youth culture." This culture is heavily materialistic and derived mainly from the adult world and the commercial media. It has its own cultural heroes, made up of rock and film stars and prominent athletes, and its own preoccupations—cars, clothes, being part of the crowd, being physically attractive. As a result, many adolescents spend little time with their families. With more money of their own, whether from earnings, an allowance, or illegal activity, adolescents do not need to go home even for dinner; they can buy their meals at a fast-food place.

Often parents become perplexed, even angry, as they feel their authority weakened and their values challenged. They may be confused about their roles in the lives of their adolescent children and lack guidance about how to proceed. They may find very little consensus, even at the community level, about the values and behavior appropriate for adolescents.

ADOLESCENTS NEED THEIR FAMILIES

Compared to families with young children, families with adolescents are neglected in community programs and public policies. Little work has been done to strengthen support networks for middle-class families during the critical transition from childhood to adulthood. Still less attention has gone into strengthening networks for families that live in poverty. Although an industry of books, videos, and experts exists for parents with young children, much less information is available to parents with adolescent children. A social consensus holds that knowledge about infant and child development is critical to a child's future. No such consensus yet exists in defining the knowledge parents should have about the adolescent years or about their roles during that critical period. To the contrary, many parents mistakenly believe they should get out of the way when their children reach adolescence, letting them become instant adults!

But this attitude ignores the fact that the transition to adulthood takes place over a period of years. Young adolescents still have a lot of growing and learning to do; they still need the supportive guidance of their parents and kin. Although adolescents are moving toward independence, they still are intimately tied to their families, which are much more important to them than they usually admit or even understand. This close connection is essential for young adolescents. Strong family relationships can be a potent force to help them deal with the radically transformed conditions of contemporary life.

A poignant response of young people to questions about why they join gangs is that these groups become the families they never had. This response is compelling testimony to a fundamental human need for close, reliable relationships within a supportive, protective group that confers respect and identity and recognizes competence.[2] This is what many gangs do, although often at the price of strict conformity to norms that tend to be antisocial and dangerous.

In survey after survey, young adolescents from all ethnic and economic backgrounds lament their lack of parental attention and guidance in making educational and career decisions, in forming adult values, and in assuming adult roles.[3] Their responses are supported by fifteen years of research on families and adolescents, from midwestern farms undergoing economic dislocation to African American neighborhoods of concentrated poverty.[4]

The conclusions drawn from this research are that adolescents develop best when they have a supportive family life characterized by warmth and mutual respect; by the serious and sustained interest of their parents in their lives; by parental responsiveness to their changing cognitive and social capacities; by the articulation of clear standards linked to discipline and close supervision; by the communication of high expectations for achievement and ethical behavior; and by democratic, constructive ways of dealing with conflict.[5] Such a family atmosphere can provide powerful protection against the risks of engaging in unhealthy practices and antisocial behavior as well as against poor health, particularly depression.

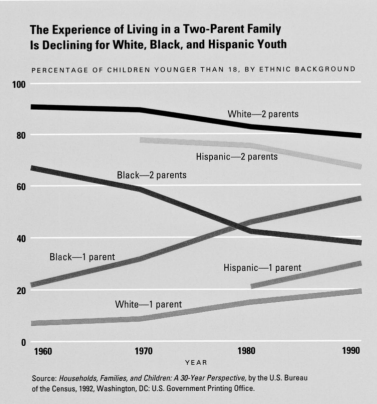

The Experience of Living in a Two-Parent Family Is Declining for White, Black, and Hispanic Youth

PERCENTAGE OF CHILDREN YOUNGER THAN 18, BY ETHNIC BACKGROUND

White—2 parents

Hispanic—2 parents

Black—2 parents

Black—1 parent

Hispanic—1 parent

White—1 parent

YEAR

Source: *Households, Families, and Children: A 30-Year Perspective,* by the U.S. Bureau of the Census, 1992, Washington, DC: U.S. Government Printing Office.

Many adults erroneously believe that hostility and conflicts between parents and their teenage children are inevitable, and that parents should disengage or detach from them in the interest of fostering adolescents' need for autonomy. Yet families who have good relations with their adolescents find they can usually negotiate a balance that satisfies the young person's growing desire for autonomy within the context of interdependence, despite normal intergenerational tensions.[6] Continuity and change can coexist in the bonds between adolescents and parents, along with much shared love and commitment.

Professionals who work with adolescents also have had misconceptions about relationships between adolescents and their families. A previous generation of studies, which focused on troubled parent-adolescent relationships, emphasized the alienation of adolescents from families as inevitable. The perspective drawn from these studies overlooks the potential of families to promote good health, high educational achievement, and ethical values for future adult responsibilities. It has discouraged education, health, and youth-development professionals from seeking ways to strengthen families in their critical role during the second decade of their children's lives.

STRENGTHENING PARENTS' ROLE DURING THE CRITICAL TRANSITION OF EARLY ADOLESCENCE

During early adolescence, three approaches—parent involvement in middle grade schools, parent peer support groups, and parental guidance on healthy adolescent development—can be helpful as parents renegotiate relationships based on the changing needs and capacities of both parties. These approaches can be incorporated into any number of settings: the first two in schools, religious institutions, and community and youth organizations; the latter wherever preventive health-care services are available to adolescents.

These three approaches to supporting parents during their children's transition into adolescence are most appropriate for families who have adequate financial resources. For families experiencing financial hardship or living in high-risk situations, family support approaches must be expanded to address the economic, social, and cultural factors that constrain the capacities of these families to carry out their essential protective and guiding functions.[7]

SUSTAINING PARENT INVOLVEMENT INTO THE MIDDLE GRADES

As children become young adolescents, the percentage of parents who are actively involved in school activities declines. Approximately three-quarters of American parents report high or moderate involvement in schools when their children are eight to ten years of age. By the time their children reach age sixteen, however, only 50 percent of parents report such involvement.[8]

Parents who want their children to do well in school must maintain their close involvement in their children's education from the elementary through the middle and high school years. Yet parents who try to remain involved often encounter barriers to their participation as their children progress to middle and high school. Existing school practices, including policies and teacher attitudes, have long accepted the absence and often discouraged the involvement of parents beyond the elementary school years.

Although schools that recognize the importance of parental involvement beyond the elementary school years are relatively rare, their numbers are slowly growing.[9] Schools can engage parents of adolescents in several productive ways.[10] They can:

■ Organize parent education and support groups to learn about normal changes during adolescence

■ Exchange information about ways to guide adolescents and help shape a community of shared values about appropriate behavior

■ Inform parents about programs and students' progress on a regular basis

■ Provide specific suggestions for ways in which parents can assist with homework and other learning activities, including community youth service

■ Involve parents as volunteers in schools

■ Include parents in school governance committees

■ Create partnerships among schools, parents, and key community organizations in joint responsibility for adolescents' educational achievement and healthy development

■ Create family resource centers that provide educational programs for parents, including computer literacy, job-employment counseling, English as a second language, health promotion, and citizenship classes.

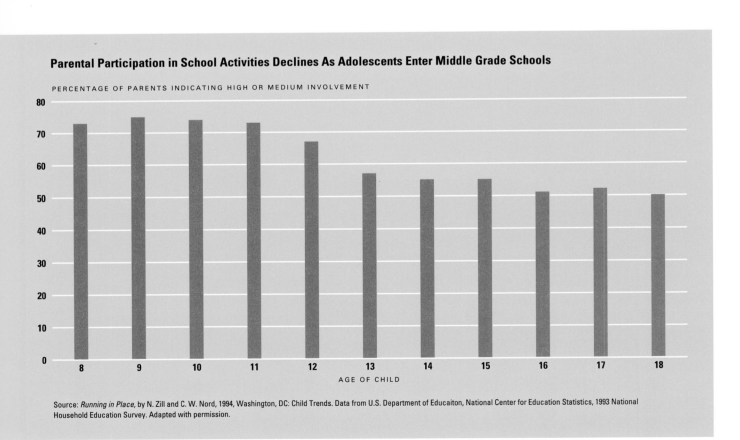

Parental Participation in School Activities Declines As Adolescents Enter Middle Grade Schools

PERCENTAGE OF PARENTS INDICATING HIGH OR MEDIUM INVOLVEMENT

AGE OF CHILD

Source: *Running in Place,* by N. Zill and C. W. Nord, 1994, Washington, DC: Child Trends. Data from U.S. Department of Educaiton, National Center for Education Statistics, 1993 National Household Education Survey. Adapted with permission.

If significant progress is to be made in improving the educational performance of teenage students, meaningful changes in the attitudes and practices of teachers and principals toward the involvement of parents will be required. The professional preparation of educators should include course work and practical experience about ways to foster parental participation in the schools and parental support for their adolescents' education.

PARENT PEER SUPPORT GROUPS

Parent peer support and education groups, in which participants share information and experience about handling the transition from childhood to adolescence, are important means of strengthening relationships between adolescents and their families. In these groups, parents can learn about normal adolescent development, how to improve their communication skills, ways to renegotiate the parent-adolescent relationship, how to set and enforce limits, and where to find resources in the community. In low-income communities, these groups also can assist parents in gaining access to health care, adult education, including literacy classes, and job training and placement.[11]

Peer support groups also can help parents cope with midlife changes. Midlife can be a difficult time for parents of growing adolescents. Parents may be struggling with their own marital relationship, issues related to aging and work, and the illness and frailty of elderly parents.[12]

Mutual aid groups of this kind can be formed in diverse communities and reach a large number of families in an efficient way. If they become sufficiently widespread, such groups could clarify and strengthen community norms regarding parent-adolescent relationships and desired behaviors in the adolescent peer group. By stressing prevention by meeting adolescents' developmental needs, such groups can generate positive attitudes and skills (in both adolescents and adults) that extend beyond the home and family.

> I'd like to design a building rather than fight. I'd like to be an architect or something like that. I've had a nice life so far, for eleven years, but I wish everybody would pay more attention to kids. That's something we really need. Sometimes grown-ups pay attention, but not a lot. They're kind of all wrapped up in their jobs and they don't really pay attention to little children. I think it wouldn't be so violent if people paid attention.
>
> RAOUL, 11

PROSPECTIVE GUIDANCE TO PARENTS ON ADOLESCENT TRANSITIONS

The Guidelines for Adolescent Preventive Services of the American Medical Association (AMA) recommend that parents or other caregivers of adolescents receive prospective information and guidance on early, middle, and late adolescence as part of adolescents' annual health examinations.[13] Currently, such guidance to parents of infants and young children is accepted health practice, but it is not widely recognized as a need for parents of adolescents. During these visits, the AMA recommends that parents learn about:

■ Normal adolescent physical, sexual, and emotional development

■ The signs and symptoms of disease and emotional distress

■ Ways to promote healthy adolescent adjustment

■ Ways to prevent potential problems (e.g., how to help adolescents drive responsibly, how to monitor social and recreational activities, and how to restrict sexual behavior and the use of tobacco, alcohol, and other drugs).

KEY OPPORTUNITIES FOR POLICY REASSESSMENT

Legislation and public policies do not yet recognize the potential of families to make a difference in their adolescents' health and educational outcomes. To encourage and support parents' and other adults' constructive roles in the lives of adolescents, changes in policies, programs, and laws are essential.

■ **Schools, cultural, arts, religious, and youth organizations and health-care agencies in the community should examine the extent to which they involve parents in activities with adolescents and should develop ways to engage parents and adolescents in mutually rewarding activities.**[14] There may be instances when parents should be explicitly excluded (e.g., adolescent peer support groups), but the reasons for such exclusion should be clear.

■ **Professionals such as teachers, nurses, social workers, physicians, psychologists, youth development specialists, and others who work with adolescents must be prepared to work not only with individual adolescents but also with their families.**

■ **Employers should extend to parents of young adolescents the workplace policies now available for those with young children, including flex time, job sharing, telecommuting, and part-time work with benefits.** Such family-friendly workplace policies allow parents to become more involved in middle and high schools, to serve as volunteers in community organizations, and to spend more time with their teens.

■ **Community institutions such as business, schools, and youth organizations should become involved in providing after-school programs.** After-school programs for elementary-age children are growing, but those for young adolescents remain scarce. More high-quality, community-based programs for adolescents are needed during the after-school, weekend, and vacation hours.[15] Parents' assumption that young adolescents are old enough to be without adult supervision or planned activities must change to reflect what young adolescents say they need.

■ **Congress should consider extending the child care tax credit to the early adolescent period, ages ten to fourteen.** Although such an extension raises complex issues, the value of such a policy change is clear. Families can benefit from placing their young adolescents in high-quality after-school programs to the same degree that they now benefit from placing young children in child care and early childhood centers and elementary-age children in after-school programs. The cost savings obtained by keeping in place the current cap on the upper age limit for child care tax credits should be reevaluated by comparing them to the costs of treating problems of substance abuse and teen pregnancy, problems that often are the result of inadequate supervision.

Characteristics of Supportive Families

Contrary to conventional wisdom, young adolescents want to have a good relationships with their parents. They tend to seek regular contact with them and other caring adults. Adolescents also *need* these close relationships. Supportive families are very important in enhancing both educational achievement and good health. Research has clarified some major characteristics of families that are effectively supportive.

■ **They combine warmth and authoritativeness.** Parents should encourage family relationships based on mutual respect and democratic principles, communicate their high expectations for achievement and ethical behavior, provide firm discipline, and balance monitoring and supervision with their adolescents' desire for independence. They also should acknowledge and adapt to their adolescents' changing cognitive and social capacities.

■ **They get involved in their adolescents' education.** Parents often think they no longer need to be involved with their children's schooling after their children have left elementary school. But research shows that parents can enhance adolescents' education by remaining actively engaged in the schooling process and other aspects of their children's lives. Participation in parental support groups may help parents share experiences and understand their growing adolescents.

■ **They develop constructive ways of handling conflict.** Disagreements are a normal part of family life. As long as conflict occurs within the context of good parent-adolescent relationships, it is not necessarily detrimental. In fact, conflict has an important role to play in bringing differences of opinion out into the open so that they can be discussed and resolved. Constructive conflict resolution helps adolescents develop good psychosocial and interpersonal skills.

■ **They seek active involvement with their young adolescents beyond education.** Most working parents complain about not having enough time to spend with their adolescents. This lack of time is detrimental to both parents and adolescents. Without the supervision of responsible adults, adolescents are vulnerable to negative peer pressure. Changes in workplace policies and practices can help forestall the power of such influences. Effective parents actively seek favorable settings in which to spend mutually enjoyable time with their children.

SOURCE

Small, S.A. (1990). *Preventive programs that support families with adolescents*. Washington, DC: Carnegie Council on Adolescent Development.

American Businesses Invest in Young Adolescents

More parents of young adolescents must find ways to balance their work and family responsibilities today than ever before. As the number of dual-earner and single-parent families continues to rise, parents who work outside the home find few safe, high-quality programs to provide structure and adult guidance for their young adolescents after school and during vacations and holidays. Finding quality care is even more difficult for parents who work nontraditional hours, in workplaces that operate twenty-four hours a day. In response to the growing needs of parents, a number of American corporations have begun to diversify their dependent benefits programs to support parents of young adolescents.

REACHING OUT TO FAMILIES

Some major employers have joined forces to provide activities for their employees' young adolescents during the out-of-school hours. The American Business Collaboration for Quality Dependent Care (ABC) is a coalition formed in 1992 by 137 corporations (expanded to 156 companies by the end of 1994), to assist employees in finding reliable, local care for their dependents. To address the lack of programs for young adolescents when schools are not in session, the ABC provided funding for the creation of adventure camps, ropes and challenge courses, and science and technology camps.

"WE HAVE FUN BUILDING THINGS"

To help parents find attractive and educational alternatives for their young adolescents, members of ABC funded the development of summer science and technology (Sci/Tech) camps for ten- to fourteen-year-olds, where campers learn about computer graphics, solar power, and architecture. Members of ABC see the camps as an investment in the future and as a child care solution for their employees with young adolescents. The camps open early and stay open late to fit parents' work schedules. Attendance at these camps is not limited to the children of the sponsoring corporations—the parents of 64 percent of the campers at STAR (Science and Technology Adventure Researchers) Camp in South Brunswick, New Jersey, work for other companies. The Sci/Tech camps reach out to girls and to minorities, who are traditionally underrepresented in science and math camps. In New Jersey, two new Sci/Tech camps emphasize hands-on science experience for young adolescents, who are challenged to ask questions, make scientific predictions, and plan for their futures.

At the STAR Camp, sponsored by several ABC partners including AT&T, IBM, and Johnson & Johnson, the sessions held at the camp's Liberty Science Center are the highlight of each day. Campers go on field trips to explore the working world of science. They meet scientists, engineers, and technicians at Mobil Research and Development's Water Toxicology Lab and other area companies. There, campers are scientists for a day, wearing lab coats and goggles and preparing real experiments. Such experiences show young adolescents that what they learn in the classroom during the school year and at camp during the summer does apply to the "real world." According to one camper, "STAR Camp is much better than other camps because you get to play computers and go to more field trips than other camps."

BALANCING WORK AND FAMILY LIFE

Other companies, either in addition to or independent of ABC, have their own work and family divisions that develop programs to help employees balance work and family life. IBM, for example, offers its 150,000 employees (60 percent of whom are part of a dual-income couple, 30 percent of whom have children who require supervision, and 5 percent of whom are single parents) several Work and Personal Life Balance Programs. These programs provide flexible leave and telecommuting options to parents.

To develop ways to make flexible schedules available to parents and to reduce absenteeism and tardiness, Marriott International, AT&T, Stride Rite, and Hewlett-Packard formed Flex Group. Flex Group members believe that flexible schedules make good business sense: employees who have schedule flexibility are more productive and are loyal to their companies.

Marriott International's Work-Life Department has developed alternative working arrangements for their employees who are parents of young adolescents. In addition to job sharing, condensed work weeks, and telecommuting, the department offers informational videos and materials on parenting, child care, and other concerns to help parents balance work and family demands. Marriott also established a bilingual and confidential Associate Resource Line (ARL) pilot service. Staffed by master's-level social workers, ARL provides twenty-four-hour counseling and advice to employees about concerns that arise from balancing work and family. ARL currently serves about thirteen of Marriott's units; in 1995, the service is expected to be expanded to include seventy-five more units.

Toyota Motor Manufacturing in Georgetown, Kentucky, operates a twenty-four-hour child development center on site for children whose parents work round-the-clock shifts. The center arranges for school-age children to be picked up at school and dropped off at the center, where they receive assistance with their homework from 4:30 to 6:30, eat dinner, and go to bed at 9:00 on school nights. During the summer, the center runs a full-day summer camp. About 60 percent of the children enrolled in the camp are between the ages of ten and thirteen.

THE FUTURE

The companies of ABC are winning praise for their efforts to respond to the needs of their employees' families. These innovators also are inspiring other companies to follow their lead. As more and more young adolescents are part of families where both parents or guardians work full time outside the home, the availability of flexible work options and quality out-of-school programs becomes increasingly important. These companies demonstrate that the extension of dependent care benefits to parents of young adolescents is a viable way to increase parents' productivity.

CONNECTING FAMILIES WITH SUPPORTIVE COMMUNITY INSTITUTIONS

Young adolescents are seeking to build new strengths. Yet these new strengths typically are constructed on existing foundations. Adolescents want new interdependence with parents and other relatives, not a rupture in the name of independence. To build this interdependence takes time, sensitivity, resilience and, above all, the persistence of parents even in the face of provocation or disappointment.

Unfortunately, there are circumstances in both affluent and economically disadvantaged families in which parents are unable or unwilling to fulfill their responsibilities to their children. Parents may be depressed and lacking in hope; they may be substance abusers who physically or emotionally neglect or abuse their children. The provision of family-like or -equivalent functions by a wide range of individuals and groups beyond the family is essential for adolescents to survive these nonsupportive situations.

Although there is no easy substitute for a deeply caring parent, adolescents cannot thrive unless some person or group steps in to meet their developmental needs. Family-like functions can be provided by committed, long-term mentors; sensitive, trustworthy advisors in middle schools; close relationships with kin in an extended family network; and other stable, mature adults in youth and community organizations. Parents who are themselves experiencing difficulties may benefit from family support, including substance abuse treatment and counseling in health and community agencies, including schools.[16] The next four chapters of this report are devoted to community institutions that support families in their vital functions—and that at times must substitute for them.

■ ■ ■ ■ ■ ■ ■ ■

Further Reading

Epstein, J. L. (1995). School/ family/ community partnerships: Caring for the children we share. *Phi Delta Kappan, 76*, 701–712.

Feldman, S. S., & Elliot, G. R. (Eds.). (1990). *At the threshold: The developing adolescent.* Cambridge, MA: Harvard University Press.

Hauser, S. T., Powers, S. I., & Noam, G. G. (1991). *Adolescents and their families: Paths of ego development.* New York: Free Press.

Zill, N., & Nord, C. W. (1994). *Running in place: How American families are faring in a changing economy and an individualistic society.* Washington, DC: Child Trends, Inc.

CHAPTER SIX

Educating Young Adolescents for a Changing World

If it were possible to reach any consensus about high-priority solutions to our society's problems, a good education throughout the first two decades of life would be a prime candidate. Every modern nation must develop the talents of its entire population if it is to be economically vigorous and socially cohesive. Education is a key ingredient in an individual's success as well: for example, well-educated and healthy young adults are rarely found in our burgeoning prison population.

In contemporary societies, a significant transition occurs during early adolescence when a young person moves from elementary school to middle grade or junior high school. Often this move is from a neighborhood school, where the student has spent most of the day in one classroom with the same teacher and classmates, to a larger school farther from home, with many different classes and teachers. This transition coincides with a time when most adolescents are experiencing profound physical, cognitive, and emotional changes. The juxtaposition of these changes adds up to a situation in which the capacities of young adolescents to cope are severely tested.[1]

A middle grade education designed specifically to meet the developmental needs of young adolescents can provide potent intellectual challenge and social support that both enhance educational achievement and promote healthy development during adolescence. It can link research on child and adolescent development with research on education in daily practice.

Although education in the middle grades clearly has the potential to make a positive difference in the futures of students, this level of education was largely ignored in the educational reform movement of the 1980s. In a landmark report, *Turning Points: Preparing Youth for the 21st Century*, published in 1989, the Carnegie Council on Adolescent Development took a major step toward filling this serious gap. It reinforced an emerging movement to create developmentally appropriate schools for young adolescents and to strengthen their education through new linkages among schools, families, communities, and health organizations. Today, with the support of a major grant-making program of Carnegie Corporation, called the Middle Grade School State Policy Initiative (MGSSPI), the core recommendations of this report are being extensively implemented in fifteen states, involving nearly one hundred schools throughout the United States and the Commonwealth of Puerto Rico.

In *Turning Points,* the Council asserted that a volatile mismatch exists between the organization and curriculum of middle grade schools (junior, intermediate, or middle schools) and the intellectual, emotional, and interpersonal needs of young adolescents.[2] It then proposed a set of high-aspiration but not utopian reforms for the middle grades.

The new middle grade school, the report stated, should be oriented to meet the essential requirements of healthy adolescent development. It must have teachers who are specially prepared to work with young adolescents. It should have curricula that provide the information, skills, and motivation for adolescents to learn about themselves and their widening world. It should have a mutual aid ethic among teachers and students, manifest in team teaching, cooperative learning, and academically supervised community service. The report's prescriptions would have applicability to the earlier grades and beyond the middle grade schools as well.

At the heart of *Turning Points* is a set of eight principles for transforming the education of young adolescents. The principles were created by integrating current research knowledge with the experience and judgment of eminent researchers, educators, policymakers, and advocates for children and youth. The principles are:

CREATE COMMUNITIES FOR LEARNING

Many American middle grade schools are large, impersonal institutions. Opportunities for teachers to develop the stable personal relationships with students that are essential to teaching them well and to provide guidance during the occasionally turbulent period of early adolescence often are nonexistent. Unacceptably large schools can be brought to human scale by creating schools-within-schools or "houses" within the school and then dividing these subunits into smaller "teams" of teachers and students. Such arrangements enable each student to receive a significant amount of individual attention within a supportive group that each must have to thrive.

TEACH A CORE OF COMMON KNOWLEDGE

Much of learning and the development of solutions to complex problems lies in the ability to integrate disparate bodies of information. Yet in many middle grade schools, the curriculum is so fragmented by subject matter that students have virtually no opportunity to make connections among ideas in different disciplines. Even in classes, middle grade students often are not challenged intellectually, reflecting the persistent misapprehension that young adolescents generally are incapable of critical or "higher-order" thinking.

A primary task for middle grade educators, especially as part of teaching teams, is to identify the most important principles and concepts within each academic discipline and to concentrate their efforts on integrating these main ideas to create a meaningful interdisciplinary curriculum. To make such a curriculum possible, teachers must embrace the idea that less is more—that is, the current emphasis in the curriculum on coverage of a large quantity of information must yield to an emphasis on the depth and quality of understanding of a limited number of major concepts in each subject area.

Creating Powerful Interdisciplinary Curricula

The creation of thoughtful interdisciplinary curricula and learning strategies is time consuming and intellectually challenging. It requires significant effort by the middle grade interdisciplinary teaching team. Teachers may be fearful that important concepts from their subject of specialization will be lost within an integrated approach or that they will be unable to satisfy state and local requirements to cover masses of information.

Despite these difficulties, many middle schools have created effective interdisciplinary curricula, including some remarkable schools serving disadvantaged students. One example is the Graham and Parks School in Cambridge, Massachusetts, which focuses on interdisciplinary project learning and portfolio assessment. Its humanities program, which combines language arts and social studies, builds curricula around concepts that are important in students' lives—for example, power and authority, individual and group responsibility, and conflict.

The school's humanities curriculum is structured around some overarching questions: What is courage? What does it mean to be a hero? Why do individuals take action to change and improve the world around them? To explore these questions, students focused in-depth on the Holocaust and the civil rights movement, as well as historical and present-day issues in the local community. The curriculum strongly emphasizes primary source material, oral history, journal writing, process and peer review writing, small-group and individual project construction, media use, and other interactive approaches.

Students at Graham and Parks also study acting and write plays. The last months of a recent school year were spent creating a student-written and -acted play that highlights the concepts and themes studied within the interdisciplinary approach. The play was performed for the school, parents, and other middle school students and educators across the city.

All students are required to maintain a portfolio containing draft and finished written work, photographs of three-dimensional projects (such as sculptures), videotapes of all presentations and exhibitions, and art work. At the end of the year, students assemble their portfolios, create a table of contents, and write a cover essay explaining their portfolio's contents and reflecting on their learning for the year. Students present their portfolios to a panel consisting of one or two prominent people from outside the school and their teacher. The portfolio and presentation are rated according to a previously agreed upon scale.

Graham and Parks school continues to have the highest scores on state tests and the widely used California Achievement Test of any middle school in the city. The school also has the largest waiting list of families wishing to enroll their children.

Integrating Science with Health

HUMBIO, an Interdisciplinary Life Sciences Curriculum for the Middle Grades

The weakest link in middle grade school reform has been the lack of appropriate curricula that provide the information, skills, and motivation for adolescents to learn about themselves and their widening world. One such curriculum development initiative over the past six years has focused on a life sciences curriculum for the middle grades. A life sciences curriculum matched to the needs and interests of young adolescents can provide them with essential concepts in biology and can relate these concepts to problems that students encounter in their daily lives. Study in the life sciences can stimulate the natural curiosity of young adolescents, who have reason to be especially interested in growth and development, as they are themselves in the midst of the early adolescent growth spurt that is one of the most striking developmental experiences of the entire life span. They are already asking, "What's happening to my body? How does the human body work anyway?" Therefore, it makes sense for them to address growth and development, particularly their own, scientifically.

The Human Biology Middle Grades Curriculum, developed and tested by Stanford University scientists in collaboration with middle grade teachers across the country, integrates the study of ecology, evolution, and genetics; physiology, human development (intellectual, psychological, and social); society and culture; and health and safety. It not only engages the average middle grade student in science but also helps simultaneously promote healthy behavior for life. The decision-making component of the curriculum connects with life skills training. It teaches skills in decision making and the capacity to draw upon information carefully, not to jump to conclusions but to be deliberate in considering the meaning of the information for one's own life.

In our current world, it is virtually impossible to be a fully healthy, productive, active citizen without some basic understanding of science. Yet students alienated from school as adolescents rarely achieve a science education higher than the most elementary level. HUMBIO is based on the experience of Stanford's twenty-five-year-old undergraduate program in human biology. It provides young people with a unique, systematic curriculum that attempts to capture their interest in their own development and allow them to apply their knowledge of the life sciences to their own health and to the social, behavioral, and family challenges they face as adolescents.

Much of the current middle grade school reform efforts rely on interdisciplinary "teaming" of teachers—involving science, mathematics, English, and social studies. The HUMBIO curriculum is founded on the premise that interdisciplinary teaching improves the student's understanding of and interest in the subject. The entire two-year HUMBIO curriculum consists of twenty-four units, and schools may choose among them. The units begin with "The Changing Body, Reproduction, and Sexuality" and move to "Genetics," "The Nervous System," "The Life of Cells," "From Cells to Organisms: Human Development," "The Circulatory System," "Breathing," and "Digestion and Nutrition." They seek to show what is meant by becoming an adult, the individual's place in the family, in the community, and in the biological world.

In using HUMBIO, teachers work cooperatively from the perspectives of their individual disciplines toward imparting a central lesson. For example, when a unit in science class deals with the impact of food and drugs on circulation, the physical education teacher makes the connection between lung function and smoking. Students study the relationships among circulation, breathing, food intake, and drugs. The study of health includes decisions regarding smoking, an analysis of different ways of planning menus, the facts behind eating disorders, and ways to reduce stress. One lesson helps students understand how drugs affect their bodies. Seventh graders at Egan Intermediate School in Los Altos, California, examine the effects of adrenaline, which the body produces when stimulated by cocaine use, on metabolism by watching brine shrimp react to a single drop through a microscope. Students have an opportunity to discuss the ideas demonstrated in the experiment, to ask questions, and to offer solutions. Teachers report that the curriculum makes science more meaningful for all students and that the integrated approach helps increase girls' comfort with science.

In mathematics, students learn the meaning of ratios, percentages, and probabilities. They may calculate the amount of smoke inhaled by a cigarette smoker, and the amount of second-hand smoke inhaled by nonsmokers in a shared work space. They may be asked to figure the actual financial cost to an individual who smokes one pack a day from age seventeen to seventy. Throughout all phases of the unit, students keep journals to describe their observations and findings. In physical education, students examine the effects of their activities on their heart beat, pulse, and blood pressure as well as the impact of smoking on lung functioning. At the end of the unit, students plan and cook a nutritionally balanced lunch.

English teachers may encourage students to read books related to what they have observed in science class; social studies teachers may deal with the impact of biological and other scientific developments on society or explore the changing views about human biology at different stages of history. Talking about evolution may involve science, history, and social studies teachers.

HUMBIO has been thoroughly field-tested at schools selected for their diversity in student population and geographic location. HUMBIO teachers have been trained in three summer institutes at Stanford. From the beginning, teachers were full partners in the project. They favored the development of a series of curriculum units or modules, not a textbook on human biology. They suggested that the units should contain an abundance of hands-on activities that would allow students to engage in the process of scientific investigation, provide better access to these materials for lower-achieving students who often get left out of more traditional science courses driven by long vocabulary lists, and make direct connections between the science presented and the health and well-being of the student.

At the test sites, teachers and students report that the activities and their applications to health, social, and environmental issues have been the most successful features of the HUMBIO units. The curriculum does not necessarily replace a life science curriculum in the middle school, but instead schools may chose the HUMBIO units that fit their particular needs. Schools may also choose to use some of the HUMBIO units for their health requirement. Teachers report that the practical applications of the lessons help students make personal health decisions based on scientific knowledge and understand the consequences of their actions. Addison-Wesley, a publisher, will produce the units and their related teacher manuals. The first ten units will be available to schools and for review by state adoption committees in the spring of 1996. The HUMBIO curriculum demonstrates that science is a field of study in which all students can be involved and that students learn best when their teachers connect what is learned in school with the real world.

SOURCE

Heller, H. C. (1993). The need for a core, interdisciplinary, life-sciences curriculum in the middle grades. In R. Takanishi (Ed.), *Adolescence in the 1990s: Risk and opportunity* (pp.189–196). New York: Teachers College Press.

In *Turning Points* schools, curriculum and instruction combine to stimulate interest in the sciences, especially in the life sciences, as a way of both sharpening intellectual capacities and of enabling young people to evaluate potentially high-risk behavior in relation to the body's functional systems. The life sciences, dealing with living organisms and life processes, offer a distinct opportunity for young adolescents to cultivate an early affinity for science and to become motivated to develop healthy practices based on scientific understanding.

Turning Points schools also consider community service or "service learning" to be an integral part of the core curriculum. As a form of project-based learning, community service promotes critical thinking about real-world problems, while allowing young people to make a valued social contribution, develop key skills for employment, and build self-esteem through solid accomplishment.

PROVIDE OPPORTUNITY FOR ALL STUDENTS TO SUCCEED

One of the most troubling aspects of middle grade schools—and of American education in general—is the inequitable distribution among youth of opportunities to learn. One way in which this occurs is through "tracking," a system by which students are assigned to a class based on their past academic achievement. Tracking is almost universal in American middle grade schools. It was implemented to reduce the heterogeneity of students in a class, thus, in theory, enabling teachers to adjust the level of instruction to match students' knowledge and skills. In practice, wide disparities in the quality of instruction and the competence of teachers are common between the high and low tracks.

Middle grade educators can do a great deal to teach students of diverse ability. One well-researched instructional method is cooperative learning.[3] Numerous studies on cooperative learning demonstrate that in mixed-ability learning groups high achievers deepen their understanding of material by explaining it to lower achievers who, in turn, benefit by receiving help as needed from their peers. Cooperative learning has been shown to help students learn course material faster, retain it longer, and develop critical reasoning power more rapidly than they would working alone. Cooperative learning also requires students to get to know and to work with classmates of different ethnic, racial, and cultural backgrounds, which sets the stage for students to negotiate successfully the requirements of adult work life and of citizenship in a pluralistic society.

STRENGTHEN TEACHERS AND PRINCIPALS

Currently, teachers and principals at all levels of elementary and secondary education, including middle schools, are severely limited in their ability to make decisions about their own practice. They are bound by tradition, by their own educational experiences, and by the specific rules and regulations of federal, state, and local educational agencies. Yet these same professionals increasingly are being asked to develop and implement innovations that will produce high levels of achievement among a much larger proportion of students than is currently the norm.

States and school districts should give teachers and principals the authority to transform middle grade schools. Teachers, principals, and other members of the school staff know more about how to do their jobs than those far removed from the classroom. Teachers especially need control over the ways they meet curricular goals. Creation of governance committees composed of teachers, administrators, support staff, parents, and representatives from community organizations is one way to make schools more effective.

PREPARE TEACHERS FOR THE MIDDLE GRADES

Most teachers in middle grade schools are not now specifically educated to teach young adolescents.[4] Although there are a few graduate education programs that prepare middle grade teachers, most teachers are educated either as elementary or secondary school teachers.

To orient teachers effectively for the middle grades, teacher education programs must prepare teachers to teach as part of a team, to design and assess meaningful interdisciplinary curricula, to participate in decisions that promote continuous school improvement, and especially to understand adolescent development. Teachers' professional education, and that of administrators, must also include specific training in working with students and families of various income, ethnic, and racial backgrounds.

IMPROVE ACADEMIC PERFORMANCE THROUGH BETTER HEALTH AND FITNESS

Middle grade schools often do not have the support of health and social service agencies to address young adolescents' physical and mental health. *Turning Points* calls for the establishment of developmentally appropriate health facilities for young adolescents that are related to the curriculum and to the health-promotion potential of the school environment. These centers, based in or near schools, are discussed in chapter seven.

REENGAGE FAMILIES IN THE EDUCATION OF YOUNG ADOLESCENTS

Despite the clearly documented beneficial effects of parental involvement on students' achievement in school and attitudes toward school, as noted in chapter five, parental involvement of all types declines steadily during the elementary school years.[5] By middle grade school, the home-school connection has been significantly reduced and too often is nonexistent. A key recommendation of *Turning Points* is to involve parents in decision making in significant ways. Particularly in low-income and racial- and ethnic-minority neighborhoods, parents often are considered part of the problem of educating young adolescents rather than an important potential educational resource.

Parents who are involved in planning the work of the school feel useful, develop confidence in their relations with school staff, and are more likely to attend school activities, a practice that signals to their young adolescents the importance of education. In low-income communities, parents' participation with school staff members on a governance committee can help heal the schism that often exists between families and schools.

Schools as Partners with Families and Communities

Schools can become partners with families and communities in order to strengthen and broaden their educational work. During the last fifteen years, states and communities have been developing programs to improve adolescents' access to health, social, and educational services in or near schools. Whether they are "full-service" schools or simply school-affiliated health centers, such programs represent a powerful attempt to address the scope of adolescents' needs. Some programs serve students' families as well. Drawing students and families into a variety of constructive activities, they can be especially helpful for students who are at risk of failing or dropping out.

Despite increased state and local funding, these efforts are still precarious. Without secure financing, they frequently face operational, managerial, and staffing problems. Many are remarkably successful, however. The Salome Ureña Middle Academies in Washington Heights, New York, for example, grew out of a city school district's partnership with a nonprofit community center and now provides comprehensive services to adolescents and their families. The Hanshaw Middle School in Modesto, California, grew into a community center. Although each of these programs takes a different approach, they share a common vision of community education.

SALOME UREÑA MIDDLE ACADEMIES

In a collaboration between the New York City school system and the Children's Aid Society, Salome Ureña Middle Academies, or IS 218, have invited community organizations to provide school-based programming for 1,200 students and their families since 1992. The curriculum includes the entire school day—and beyond. During "zero period," for instance, students can eat breakfast together, dance, and participate in other recreational activities. During the after-school program, more than 500 students receive tutoring designed to maximize their academic and artistic strengths and interests.

The school's family resource center, open from 8:30 a.m. to 8:30 p.m., is a valuable source of information and support for the community. Staffed by parents, social workers, and other volunteers, the center provides adult education, drug abuse prevention activities, and other forms of assistance. Because many of the neighborhood's families are of Dominican origin, the school offers an English-as-a-Second Language program, in which four hundred parents are currently enrolled. They in turn volunteer to teach their native tongue to the precinct's police officers. Next door to the resource center is a clinic that provides medical care, dental care, and referrals to students. The clinic will soon include mental health services, which will be provided by a full-time psychologist and a part-time psychiatrist.

The Children's Aid Society, which operates the school, has been inundated with requests for tours of the school and for information and assistance in establishing similar schools elsewhere. It has hosted more than five hundred visitors, and requests for visits now average three per week. To respond to these requests, a technical assistance and information clearinghouse has been established at the school to facilitate partnerships in other communities by connecting interested schools with potential local or regional partners.

HANSHAW MIDDLE SCHOOL

"Always do your personal best" is the prominently displayed motto of this community school, where the emphasis is on individuality, flexibility, responsibility, and cooperation. Established in 1991, Hanshaw Middle School aims to meet the needs of the community as well as provide educational and social opportunities for the adolescents of California's Stanislaus County. Adjacent to a recreation center, the school itself serves as the neighborhood's community center. The six buildings on the school's campus house an auto shop, a home economics lab, a gymnasium and multipurpose auditorium, laboratories, arts and crafts rooms, and state-of-the-art music rehearsal rooms. The school's library is actually a branch of the local county system.

The school also is a resource center for its students' families. Parents can take classes in parenting or computers or study for their high school equivalency degrees. Hispanic parents can receive help communicating with the school's faculty and administrators. Also on site is a center for primary health and dental care. Established by the Healthy Start Support Services for Children Act of 1991, the center features a case management team and referral service available to students and their families.

SOURCES

Dryfoos, J. G. (1994). *Full-service schools: A revolution in health and social services for children, youth, and families.* San Francisco: Jossey-Bass.

U.S. General Accounting Office (1994). *School-based health centers can expand access for children* (GAO/HEHS-95–35). Washington, DC: Author.

U.S. General Accounting Office. (1993). *School-linked human services: A comprehensive strategy for aiding students at risk of school failure* (GAO/HRD-94–21). Washington, DC: Author.

Frustrated by their inability to stem the high rates of adolescent problems and by the fact that adolescents most at risk were not making use of available services, social service professionals and leaders in community organizations in the 1980s began moving their activities to where young people are—in the schools. "Full-service schools" are major innovations in human services whose development has been led by individual states.[6] They represent a variety of school-based efforts to assist students and their families, going beyond health centers to include comprehensive youth-service programs, community schools, and family resource centers. Strengthening the academic environment in conjunction with supporting students and the basic human needs of their families is the common core of all such efforts.

School districts pay for only a few of these programs. Funding comes from outside sources, primarily states, which contract with one or more community agencies to work in partnership with the school. Each state has designed its own version of school-based services. In some states, the initiative lies in the domain of the department of education, and the focus is on preventing dropouts and promoting academic achievement. In other states, the department of health or the department of human services is the lead agency, whose goal is to reduce high-risk behavior through school-based interventions.

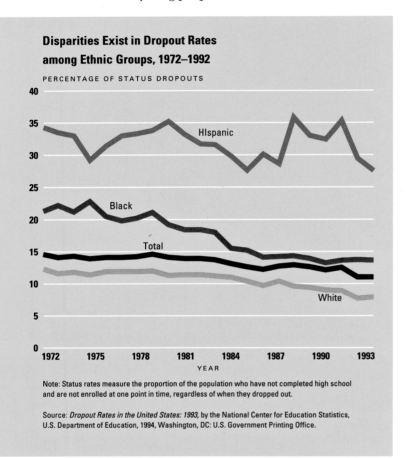

Disparities Exist in Dropout Rates among Ethnic Groups, 1972–1992

PERCENTAGE OF STATUS DROPOUTS

Hispanic

Black

Total

White

YEAR

Note: Status rates measure the proportion of the population who have not completed high school and are not enrolled at one point in time, regardless of when they dropped out.

Source: *Dropout Rates in the United States: 1993,* by the National Center for Education Statistics, U.S. Department of Education, 1994, Washington, DC: U.S. Government Printing Office.

THE MIDDLE GRADE SCHOOL STATE POLICY INITIATIVE

Turning Points marked the beginning of Carnegie Corporation's effort to stimulate nationwide reform of American middle grade schools by offering a plan of action for transforming them. In 1990, the Corporation initiated the Middle Grade School State Policy Initiative (MGSSPI), a program of grants to states (usually the state department of education) to stimulate statewide changes in middle grade educational policy and practice.[7] Designed as a "top-down, bottom-up" comprehensive reform strategy, the initiative promotes widespread implementation of the *Turning Points* reform principles through changes in state policies that encourage local schools to adopt promising practices and fosters the development of schools that serve educationally disadvantaged young adolescents, an urgent national priority.

The initiative is focused on fifteen states whose work to reform the middle grade educational policy is producing meaningful results. Most of these states have developed or are actively implementing comprehensive middle grade policy statements reflecting *Turning Points.* These statements, which have been approved by the state board of education or legislature, guide restructuring efforts statewide and, in some states, are among the criteria for state accreditation of schools, a powerful incentive for change. Several states have established a middle grade unit within the state education agency where no such unit existed before the initiative. Most of the states have established or accelerated implementation of teacher certification requirements for

middle grade teachers or made it possible to earn a special endorsement as a trained middle grade teacher. State projects have been actively involved in developing statewide middle grade curriculum and assessment frameworks, incorporating a middle grade focus into existing frameworks, and evaluating the new frameworks' usefulness in reforming classroom practice. Most projects have established strong relationships with health and other state agencies outside the education department to expand and coordinate the resources available to schools for comprehensive health programs.

To improve curriculum, instruction, and assessment under the MGSSPI, states have employed a variety of sophisticated methods, often involving a multilayered infrastructure of support. The states have developed, for example, week-long summer institutes on interdisciplinary instruction and portfolio-based assessment; on-site, professional development seminars facilitated by university faculty members; formal networks to exchange information and resources between schools; systems for identifying, training, and deploying expert consultants; and many other forms of assistance.

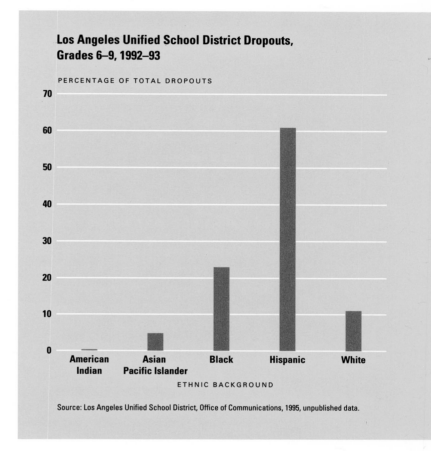

Los Angeles Unified School District Dropouts, Grades 6–9, 1992–93

PERCENTAGE OF TOTAL DROPOUTS

ETHNIC BACKGROUND

Source: Los Angeles Unified School District, Office of Communications, 1995, unpublished data.

At the local level, the MGSSPI has stimulated improvement in more than one hundred middle schools in the fifteen states. Since 1993, each state has focused its effort on creating networks of four to ten schools serving high concentrations of disadvantaged students. These schools tend to be the least effective in educating young adolescents because the most inexperienced teachers are often assigned to them, teacher and administrator turnover is extraordinarily high, low expectations for student performance prevail, and staff members have minimal access to professional development experiences that enable them to reach students who have often been poorly prepared in elementary school.

Educating students well in schools in low-income communities is also especially difficult because the young people themselves often are caught up in circumstances that make learning extremely difficult. These young adolescents, more often than more advantaged students, face

Turning Points Schools in Action

Through its Middle Grade School State Policy Initiative (MGSSPI), Carnegie Corporation of New York is implementing the *Turning Points* recommendations in nearly one hundred schools and fifteen states nationwide. Some schools stand out as having accomplished their goals against formidable challenges: their communities have few resources; adolescents have limited access to health care; or the violence and worsening social circumstances of their communities seem too overwhelming to conquer. Two schools, Turtle Mountain Community Middle School in Belcourt, North Dakota, and Morningside Middle School in Fort Worth, Texas, have met these challenges and made significant strides toward achieving middle school reform.

TURTLE MOUNTAIN COMMUNITY MIDDLE SCHOOL

Turtle Mountain Community Middle School is located on an Indian reservation in Belcourt, North Dakota. Ninety-eight percent of Turtle Mountain's 450 students in grades six through eight are American Indians of the Turtle Mountain Band of Chippewa Indians. In response to the needs of its students, many of whom come from one-parent families, Turtle Mountain has placed a special focus on mentoring and the development of social competence.

One of the longest-standing social support programs at Turtle Mountain is the Teacher-Advisor program. Each teacher is assigned a small group of students (ten to fifteen in seventh and eight grades, twenty in sixth) for which he or she is mentor, advisor, and counselor. In daily group meetings that take the place of a home room period, students learn about human development, improve their self-esteem, and build their public speaking skills. The staff at Turtle Mountain have found that these morning sessions focus the students on school and learning and help them deal with their family problems. The small group size allows the teacher-advisor to get to know his or her students well, and the student can feel part of a closely knit group of peers; if a student has a personal problem, he or she feels comfortable in approaching the teacher-advisor for advice.

A peer mediation program teaches the students how to resolve conflict peacefully. Ten peer mediators per grade are on duty, two per day, every day to help students resolve potentially serious conflicts. The peer mediators complete a training session before they begin service. They monitor the hallways with teachers to look out for fights or arguments and then ask those involved in the dispute if they can intervene. They are allowed to leave class to mediate disputes and may use the principal's office as a neutral territory. The program has cut down on discipline problems by enabling students to learn how to solve problems on their own before they require intervention by a teacher or the principal.

Through the BRIDGES program, which links six middle schools to University of North Dakota (UND) faculty for cooperative development, the teachers at Turtle Mountain can earn ten graduate credits in middle grade education free of charge. A university friend, a representative of UND, is present at all times at the school to act as a liaison between the university and the middle school. The university friend brings a knowledge base to the school's teachers and shares educational developments with them, connects teachers with other university resources, and assesses the effects of the *Turning Points* recommendations.

Teachers also participate in the Quality Council, which is composed of one teacher from each teaching team, student representatives, and parents. The Quality Council meets to discuss school policy and curriculum and to make changes. Block scheduling has allowed teachers to devote more time to planning an interdisciplinary curriculum for the students. Team teaching, as recommended in *Turning Points*, is facilitated by providing planning time every day for the teachers. The core courses (reading, math, language arts, science, and social studies) are taught in the morning. In the afternoon, students attend their related arts courses, with the art team teachers, allowing the core team teachers to meet. During this planning time, the team teachers can discuss how to integrate their individual specialties into an interdisciplinary program.

MORNINGSIDE MIDDLE SCHOOL

At Morningside Middle School in Fort Worth, Texas, Principal Odessa Ravin is proud of the progress that has been made to expand opportunities for her students to learn about the world of work. Ninety-six percent of the school's 650 sixth through eighth graders are African American. Through the district-wide Vital Link program, connecting the students to the world of work, students learn about career opportunities by visiting area hospitals, offices, and other work sites to talk with the staff and learn how school helped them achieve their professional goals. In a related effort, the Young Doctors Club brings the most promising students (those with the highest science grades) together with local physicians and other health care professionals; the majority of the 1994–95 club members are girls. The students visit a local medical school, where they attend science classes and explore the classroom laboratories. Additional field trips allow them to talk with young doctors, many of whom come from similar socio-economic backgrounds.

Morningside also offers opportunities for the parents to get involved in school activities. Twice a year it sponsors a health fair, where parents can be tested for glucose intolerance and high blood pressure and learn more about promoting their and their children's health at educational booths. In an effort sponsored in part by the Interfaith Alliance, a Practical Parent Education (PPE) course is available to parents and others responsible for raising the students. Taught by counselors and trained volunteer parents, the PPE course is designed to educate the parents about the basic *Turning Points* reform objectives of the school: parents are taught what a lesson plan is, what the school is doing to prepare their children for further secondary school education, what systemic reform is, and what kind of specialized middle grade training the teachers at Morningside receive. The PPE course is a means for families to become truly involved in their children's education.

Health services and health education are available to the students and to their parents at the school. Once a week, the Teddy Bear Clinic, a mobile clinic in an equipped van, visits Morningside with a pediatrician, a nurse, and other technicians to do routine check-ups. In addition to the clinic, a nurse or a nurse's assistant is available on campus at all times in case of illness or medical emergency. A Because We Care specialist is on staff to work with the students to help reduce substance abuse. The specialist also works with the adolescents in conflict resolution exercises. In the 1994–95 school year, incidences of conflict were 40 percent lower than the previous year.

violence in and outside the home, poor health and nutrition, drug trafficking and usage, unequal access to resources, and other negative influences. If they are nonwhite, they often are victims of discrimination. Together, these factors place economically disadvantaged youth at substantial risk of not receiving the education they need to succeed in the future. Yet disadvantaged youth are a significant proportion of students in America's public schools. Creating middle schools that can overcome the risks is the MGSSPI's highest priority.

Within *Turning Points'* comprehensive framework, reform efforts in these schools have focused on two critical areas: (1) the integration of health and education for young adolescents and (2) the reform of curriculum, instruction, and assessment. In the health arena, the majority of these schools have established or strengthened linkages to health services, both on site in the form of school-based centers, or "wellness centers," and through ties to health agencies serving adolescents in the community. Many schools have attempted to integrate health education more firmly into the middle grade curriculum, including efforts in several states to implement the Stanford University HUMBIO Curriculum.

PROMISING RESULTS OF MIDDLE GRADE REFORM

A national evaluation of the MGSSPI was begun in 1993 under the direction of Robert Felner, director of the Center for Prevention Research and Development within the University of Illinois' Institute for Governance and Public Affairs. Baseline data were collected in the spring of 1994 from nearly all the schools and now are being analyzed.

Since 1991, Felner has also been studying a group of middle grade schools in Illinois that have been implementing the *Turning Points* recommendations. This effort, called Project Initiative Middle Level (PIML), is being conducted by the Association of Illinois Middle Schools. PIML began as an initiative separate from the MGSSPI project in Illinois but will merge with it in the fall of 1995.

As in the national MGSSPI evaluation, data collected for the PIML study are primarily drawn from surveys of teachers, administrators, and students in the reforming schools. They are asked to provide information on the extent to which the structures and experiences recommended in *Turning Points* actually occur. These implementation data are compared to three outcome measures: student scores on state-administered achievement tests, teachers' rating of students' behavior, and students' own ratings of their behavior and attitudes.

Results thus far from the Illinois study show that, in forty-two schools participating in at least one year of the study since 1991, implementation of the *Turning Points* recommendations is associated with significant improvements in students' reading, mathematics, and language arts achievement. Moreover, teachers' ratings and student self-reports show that, as these proposals are implemented, students in these schools are less likely to feel alienated, fearful, or depressed in school and more likely to have high self-esteem. In thirty-one schools for which there are several years of data, the same pattern of results is found *within* schools over time. That is, as schools continue to implement *Turning Points* recommendations, achievement and behavior continue to improve.

These promising findings from the MGSSPI initiative demonstrate that, although most schools are not now designed specifically to meet the needs of young adolescents, the potential is there and can be readily tapped. Without a good education, adolescents are unprepared for life; but with the support of schools redesigned expressly to equip youth for the future, all adolescents have a better chance at educational and personal success.

▪ ▪ ▪ ▪ ▪ ▪ ▪ ▪

Further Reading

Council of Chief State School Officers. (1992). *Reform in middle grade education: Current status, future directions*. Washington, DC: Author.

Council of Chief State School Officers. (1992). *Turning points: States in action*. Washington, DC: Author.

Lewis, A. C. (1993). *Changing the odds: Middle school reform in progress, 1991–1993*. New York: Edna McConnell Clark Foundation.

Task Force on Education of Young Adolescents. (1989). *Turning points: Preparing American youth for the 21st century*. Washington, DC: Carnegie Council on Adolescent Development.

CHAPTER SEVEN

Promoting the Health of Adolescents

The continuing decline in the health status of American adolescents is deeply disturbing. Since 1960, the burden of adolescent illness has shifted from the traditional causes of disease toward the "new morbidities" associated with health-damaging behaviors, such as depression, suicide, alcohol, tobacco and drug use, sexually transmitted diseases, including HIV/AIDS, and gun-related homicides.[1]

Early adolescence is characterized by exploration and experimentation, which to some extent are developmentally appropriate and socially adaptive, even if they involve a certain amount of risk taking. But carried to extremes, these risky behaviors can impair mental and physical health. The damage may be near term and vivid, or it can explode in the long term, like a time bomb set in youth. Examples of near-term damage are sexually transmitted diseases, death or trauma from violence, and disabling accidents related to alcohol. Delayed consequences include cancer and cardiovascular disease in adult life, made more likely by high-calorie, high-fat dietary patterns, inadequate exercise, and heavy smoking. Destructive behaviors may, furthermore, result in constricting life options: a teenage mother who drops out of junior or senior high school diminishes her prospects for lifetime employment and increases the chances she will live in poverty, with its attendant risks to her own health and the health of her child.[1]

But just as early adolescence is a time when damaging patterns of behavior can begin to take hold, it also represents an optimal opportunity for the formation of healthy practices, which have equally near-term and long-term effects. Families, schools, and community organizations have an obligation, in partnership with health care professionals and organizations, to address the fundamental needs of young adolescents for information about health risks and foster the skills and motivation to avoid these risks and adopt healthy practices. Beyond this, they must create real opportunities for work and a productive adult life.

The health-related perceptions of adolescents can play a major role in motivating them to adopt healthy behavior.[2] Although their health concerns vary according to their gender, ethnicity, and socioeconomic status and change as they grow older, almost all adolescents are preoccupied with how they look and how they feel about themselves, with their relationships to their peers, and with educational pressures. Many adolescents are similarly concerned about issues of substance use, sexuality, nutrition, and exercise. By and large, they show the same tendency as adults to wishfully minimize the potentially damaging effects of their risky behavior,[3] persisting in the belief that "it can't happen to me." As a practical matter, such views should be taken into consideration in the design of appropriate supports to adolescents. If such supports ignore adolescent perceptions and preoccupations, and if they are not user-friendly, they are not likely to be sought by the very individuals who need them most.[4]

EDUCATION FOR HEALTH IN EARLY ADOLESCENCE: A ROLE FOR MIDDLE GRADE SCHOOLS

A central theme of the Council's work is the inextricable link between education and health. Adolescents in poor health have difficulty learning: for example, deficits in vision and hearing can impair the processing of information; malnutrition causes lethargy; substance abuse destroys attention to instruction. Conversely, young people fully engaged in learning tend to have good health habits and to be healthy. The relationship between education and health pertains at every level of development throughout the life span.[5]

As we have seen, a great many adolescents arrive at middle grade school with inadequate skills to cope with their great transition to adulthood. Much of what they need goes beyond the traditional curriculum offered by the public school system—a fact that is increasingly recognized by education leaders.

SCHOOLS AS HEALTH-PROMOTING ENVIRONMENTS

Middle grade schools can play a crucial role in fostering health among young adolescents. Through the curriculum, through school policy, and through the clear examples they set of health-promoting behavior, schools can encourage students to form good health habits and recognize that education and health are mutually reinforcing. In short, they can provide an environment in which good health as well as education is pursued and reinforced throughout the day, including

- The teaching of proper nutrition in the classroom and offering of nutritious food in the cafeteria

- Smoke-free buildings and programs to prevent student and staff use of tobacco

- Education on the effects of alcohol and illicit drugs on the brain and other organs

- Opportunities for exercise for all in the school community, not just varsity competition between different schools

- Emphasis on safety and the prevention of violence, including discouraging drug dealing and the carrying of weapons in and around schools.

TURNING POINTS REFORMS

Many of *Turning Points'* recommended reforms are broadly aimed at creating a health-promoting, developmentally appropriate environment in the middle schools. For example, by organizing smaller units out of large schools, they operate on a human scale. They provide sustained individual attention to students in the context of a supportive group. They foster cooperation and a mutual aid ethic among teachers and students alike, manifest in interdisciplinary team teaching, cooperative learning, and academically supervised community service. They stimulate thinking skills in the context of the sciences, especially the life sciences. They offer life skills training to develop judgment in decision making, healthy interpersonal relations, nonviolent problem solving, and the ability to use information and opportunities effectively.

THREE PREVENTIVE APPROACHES

Three kinds of programs offered by *Turning Points* schools have particular relevance for health promotion in early adolescence. These are a life sciences curriculum, life skills training, and social support programs, described in previous chapters in more detail.

- *A life sciences curriculum.* The life sciences tap into the natural curiosity of young adolescents, who are already intensely interested in the nature of life by virtue of the changes taking places in their own bodies. The life sciences can tackle growth and development, specifically addressing adolescent development in the context of a distinctly *human* biology. The study of human biology leads naturally to the scientific study of behavior and the ways in which high-risk behavior, especially in adolescence, bears on health throughout the lifetime.

- *Life skills training.* A strong underpinning of protective knowledge, derived in large part from the life sciences curriculum, is crucial but by itself is not sufficient. Such information becomes more effective when combined with training in interpersonal and decision-making skills. Having these skills can help students resist pressure from peers or from the media to engage in high-risk behaviors; increase their self control; acquire ways to reduce stress and anxiety without engaging in dangerous activity; learn how to make friends if they are isolated; and learn how to avoid violence and assert themselves effectively. Students can acquire these essential life skills through systematic instruction and practice and through role playing. Calling attention to unattractive short-term effects, such as nicotine-stained fingers, bad breath, and being out of control, can be effective in deterring tobacco and alcohol use among adolescents.

- *Social support programs.* Research evidence shows that social supports, revolving around shared values and goals, can provide powerful leverage in the promotion of health among adolescents and their families. Schools, along with community and health care organizations, can supplement the family by arranging constructive social support programs that foster health and education.

These three approaches—the life sciences curriculum, life skills training, and social supports—linked together constitute powerful facilitators of healthy adolescent development. Such a combination of influences on young adolescents can have a strong bearing on preventing serious health problems.

TARGETED APPROACHES TO HEALTH PROMOTION

To fulfill their potential for promoting health, schools must make durable linkages with other institutions. Instilling widespread knowledge and encouraging the development of healthy lifestyles in youth will require substantial changes in the way the health professions work and also in the ways they connect with schools, community organizations, and families.

Health care providers are generally viewed by adolescents as reliable sources of information about their health. Effective adolescent health care requires the active involvement of health professionals who view all clinical encounters with adolescents as opportunities for health promotion. These professionals should take the time necessary to gain the confidence of adolescents, learn to identify adolescents' problems, be willing to ask questions that might uncover alcohol and other drug abuse or sexual activity, and help them avoid dangerous behavior.

In the absence of a broad perspective on health promotion as exemplified in *Turning Points* schools, the most common approach to enhancing adolescents' health has been through categorical programs that focus on specific risks. Such categorical approaches should be complementary to the generic approach of educating youth for lifelong health. Four of these issues are selected for brief illustration here: sexuality, preparation for parenthood, violence, and drug abuse. It is important to note that other issues also deserve attention, such as mental health, nutrition, physical fitness, and injury prevention.

TOWARD RESPONSIBLE SEXUALITY

Although early adolescence clearly is not a time to become seriously engaged in sexual activity, adolescents receive conflicting messages about desirable body image and appropriate sexual behavior, especially from the media and from peers. Consequently, adolescents have a great need to understand issues related to sexuality, such as the dynamics of intimate relationships, when to become sexually active, the biological process of conception, and the risks of contracting sexually transmitted diseases, including HIV infection. Proper understanding of all these issues depends on accurate information being conveyed in sensitive and age-appropriate ways.

Young adolescents obtain their information about sexuality primarily from peers but also from family, school, television, and movies. Peer information is often inaccurate, and it may be indirectly communicated. Moreover, adolescents tend to assume erroneously that "everybody does it," even if this is not the case.

Because they have a greater potential than peers to convey accurate and age-appropriate information, families and schools are in a better position to encourage health-protective choices by young adolescents. Those adolescents who rate communication with their parents as poor are likely to have initiated sex, as well as smoking and drinking, earlier than their peers who rate communication with their parents as good.[6] Many parents, however, need help in becoming well informed about issues in reproductive health and in learning how to overcome their embarrassment about talking to their children about sexuality issues.

Adolescents should learn about human sexuality and reproduction *early*, before they become sexually active. Programs promoting sexual health should begin not later than early adolescence in middle grade schools and in youth-serving organizations. Information about preventing the transmission of the AIDS virus should also be part of health education for young adolescents. Young adolescents typically do not know, for example, that the incubation period for AIDS can be ten or more years and that mothers can transmit the virus to their offspring. Interventions should identify the sexually oriented situations that adolescents may encounter and provide life skills training on how to avoid the situation or manage it. Schools, families, and the media, through health-promoting messages and programs, can contribute to this effort.

Armed with good information and skills, young adolescents must also be motivated to make constructive choices regarding their sexuality and to prevent pregnancy—not an easy task given their inexperience and social milieu. Determining how to bring this about remains a formidable task. A recent Institute of Medicine study concluded that fewer than twenty-five programs to reduce unintended pregnancy have been carefully evaluated; of these programs, about half of them were found to be effective in the short term.[7] This is one of the many indications that research in this field has not been given adequate priority.

The vast majority of adolescent pregnancies are unintended.[8] Any sound educational approach needs to make it clear that becoming a parent at the right time, when a young person has attained the maturity to raise a family, involves more than information, birth control, and the prevention of unwanted pregnancies. Young people should be taught and public attitudes should reinforce that raising a family brings responsibilities as well as joys and that much is involved in being a reliable, competent parent.

PREPARING FOR PARENTHOOD

Another important aspect of healthy development is preparing adolescents for the time when they form families of their own in adulthood. The fulfillment of each child's potential requires a huge parental investment of time, energy, thought, caregiving, sensitivity, and money. It requires patience, persistence, understanding, and resilience in coping with adversity. All too many adolescents become pregnant only to find later that they are extremely ill prepared for the challenge of raising a child.

Young people moving toward parenthood generally have less experience caring for a child than their predecessors had. Both father and mother are likely to be in the paid labor force. With the birth of the baby, they will have to renegotiate their relationship: they will have to decide how to divide the baby care chores; what kind of flexibility they can build into their schedules; how they will handle the housework; what sort of parental leave, if any, each will take; and how they will balance work and family life.

The 1993 Carnegie Corporation report, *Starting Points: Meeting the Needs of Our Youngest Children*, emphasized the importance of preparing adolescents for responsible parenthood.[9] When people make an informed, thoughtful commitment to have children, they are more likely to be good parents. Their growing children are more likely to meet life with optimism, trust, and competence. On the other hand, when people are unprepared for the opportunities and responsibilities of parenthood, the risks to their children are serious.

The nation needs a substantial expansion of efforts to educate young people about parenthood. Families are naturally the first source of such education, but schools, places of worship, and community organizations can also be useful. Community service in child care centers provides a valuable learning experience for adolescents about what is required to raise young children. Age-appropriate, culturally sensitive education about parenthood should begin in late elementary school but no later than early adolescence. It can be a part of a life sciences curriculum or a part of health education. In either case, it must be substantial and meaningful to adolescents.

CONFLICT RESOLUTION AND VIOLENCE PREVENTION

Nearly 1 million adolescents between the ages of twelve and nineteen are victims of violent crimes each year.[10] Yet evidence is emerging that interventions can reduce or prevent young people's involvement in violence. As with the prevention of adolescent pregnancy, youth violence is not a simple problem with a single answer. To be effective, prevention requires a comprehensive approach addressing both individual and social factors.[11] It should include generic approaches that meet essential requirements for healthy adolescent development, through developmentally appropriate schools, supportive families, and youth and community organizations. A specific set of interventions that targets youth violence and enhances adolescents' ability to deal with conflict in nonviolent ways is also necessary. Policy changes, such as implementing stronger measures to restrict the availability of guns, are urgently needed, especially in light of the growing propensity of juveniles to use semiautomatic and other guns to commit crimes.[12]

One promising strategy for preventing youth violence is the teaching of conflict resolution (encompassing the management of anger and other life skills training) as part of health education in elementary and middle schools. Research indicates that conflict resolution and mediation programs can reduce violence; better results, however, are achieved with longer-term, comprehensive programs designed to address multiple risk factors.[13] Serious, in-depth conflict-resolution training over extended periods is increasingly important in a culture saturated with media and street violence. Supervised practice of conflict-resolution skills also is critical. Assertiveness, taught as a social skill, helps young people learn how to resist unwanted pressures and intimidation, resolve conflicts nonviolently, and make sound decisions about the use of weapons.

To build resources for the development of such programs, Carnegie Corporation is supporting a national network of violence prevention practitioners based at the Education Development Center, linked with a national research center on youth violence at the University of Colorado. These resources can provide a solid knowledge base and foster evaluative research in violence prevention. The two centers are joined to Mediascope, an organization addressing the depiction of violence in movies and on television.

High-risk youth in impoverished communities urgently need social support networks and life skills training. Both can be created in a wide range of existing settings, not only in schools and school-related health centers but also in community organizations, including church-related youth activities and sports programs. They work best if they foster enduring relationships with adults as well as with helpful peers. This approach can potentially promote constructive alternatives to violent groups by providing a sense of belonging, a source of enjoyable activity, a perception of opportunity, a site for mentoring, and a chance to prepare for social roles that can earn respect.

PREVENTING DRUG ABUSE

Drugs are cheaper and more plentiful today than they were a decade ago. Heroin, for example, costs less than half its 1981 street price. The United States has the highest addiction rate in its history;[14] courts and jails are bulging with drug-related cases.

Adolescents consider drugs and alcohol less harmful today than they did three years ago, and they are more accepting of drug use.[15] For many young people, the use of drugs, even the sale of drugs, constitutes an attractive path to what they perceive as adult status.

Some community-wide preventive interventions have substantially diminished the use of "gateway" substances (such as tobacco, alcohol, and marijuana) in early adolescence while enhancing personal and social competence. These efforts have been carried out using rigorous research designs on a long-term basis.[16] Several preventive programs for young adolescents have been shown to reduce drug use.[17] The learning of life skills has been usefully applied to the prevention of cigarette smoking and alcohol and marijuana use.[18] This research shows how the explicit teaching of these skills can contribute to personal and social competence and provide constructive alternatives to health-damaging behavior.

Recent studies report that when booster sessions are provided in high school, the preventive effects of early interventions are sustained through the senior year.[19] Other programs focus on the prevention of cigarette smoking, which is very important, since, aside from tobacco's "gateway" function, many casualties throughout the life span flow from the start of this addiction in early adolescence.[20] In addition, the very early start of smoking is a slippery slope to other drugs.[21] The results of well-designed, community-wide interventions are encouraging; their success suggests that social norms on drug use can be changed by systematic, intensive, and long-term efforts. A dramatic example is the recent decline in smoking reported by African American adolescents.[22]

Beyond the direct approach to substance abuse, parents, teachers, and health professionals should understand that many adolescents engage in dangerous behavior because of developmental problems such as low self-esteem, poor performance in school, depression, or inability to make careful decisions. This underscores the importance of addressing underlying factors that lead to high-risk behavior. Using drugs may be a way of feeling mature, courageous, sophisticated, or otherwise grown up. Disadvantaged youth need to be shown how individuals from comparable backgrounds have done well in legitimate ways, in sharp contrast to "successful" drug dealers involved in crime and tragedy. The provision of family-augmenting functions by community organizations can be helpful in this context.

STRENGTHENING HEALTH CARE SERVICES FOR ADOLESCENTS

An exhaustive study of adolescent health, conducted by the U.S. Congress's Office of Technology Assessment in 1991, pointed to serious barriers to establishing developmentally appropriate health services for adolescents.[23] Current services are particularly lacking in disease prevention and health-promotion services. A variety of studies and innovations in the past decade have been undertaken to overcome the barriers and to improve the delivery of health care services to adolescents.[24] These studies show what can be done, but there is a long way to go.

Barriers to Health Care Services for Adolescents

- An estimated 39.7 million Americans (15.3 percent) were without health insurance coverage during the entire 1993 calendar year.

- As many as one in seven adolescents has no health insurance; one in three poor adolescents is not covered by Medicaid, and private insurance coverage of adolescents is increasingly restricted.

- Adolescents are among those least likely to have health insurance because most adolescents, ages ten to eighteen, live with parents who are also uninsured. Adolescents whose families are poor or of Hispanic origin or whose parents have little formal education are most likely to be uninsured. In 1993, despite the existence of programs such as Medicaid and Medicare, 29.3 percent of the poor (11.5 million) had no health insurance of any kind.

- Preventive services, such as psychological and substance abuse counseling, are especially needed during adolescence and not covered by many insurance plans.

- To meet adolescents' health care needs, developmentally appropriate services must be available in a wide range of health care settings, including community health centers, school-based and school-linked health centers, physicians' offices, family planning clinics, HMOs, and hospitals. Adolescents now depend on multiple sources of care for preventive services. For approximately 80 percent of school-based clinics, for example, adolescents need another source for contraceptive health services because making the full range of contraceptives available to teens in schools is highly controversial.

- There are ethnic and cultural differences in the use of health care services. If African American and Hispanic youth had income and health insurance coverage equal to that of whites, they would still not make as many visits to the doctor. Different beliefs regarding health may influence the use of health care services; other factors include discrimination in institutional access or physician behavior; the relatively small numbers of African American and Hispanic doctors; long waiting times at neighborhood and hospital clinics; and dissatisfaction with physician behavior.

- The clinical visit provides an opportunity for health promotion and disease-prevention interventions. During this visit, physicians or other practitioners in the office setting should be able to provide health guidance, including health education, health counseling, and anticipatory guidance. This is especially important for adolescents with chronic disease and disability to maximize their function and ability to cope.

- A critical issue in the provision of health care to adolescents is that there are relatively few health care personnel who have training or experience in dealing with this age group's health problems. Training programs for physicians do not include information about and skills to serve adolescents.

SOURCES

Klein, J. D., Slap, G. B., Elster, A. B., & Cohn, S. E. (1993). Adolescents and access to health care. *Bulletin of the New York Academy of Medicine, 70,* 219–235.

Kronick, R. (1989). *Adolescent health insurance status: Analysis of trends in coverage and preliminary estimates of the effects of an employer mandate and Medicaid expansion on the uninsured.* Washington, DC: U.S. Congress, Office of Technology Assessment.

Lieu, T. A., Newacheck, P. W., & McManus, M. A. (1993). Race, ethnicity and access to ambulatory care among U. S. adolescents. *American Journal of Public Health, 83,* 960–965.

U.S. Department of Commerce, Bureau of the Census. (October 1994). *Health insurance coverage—1993.* Statistical brief (SB/94–28). Washington, DC: Author.

BROADENING HEALTH INSURANCE COVERAGE

All adolescents require preventive primary health care and treatment for health problems, yet they are likely to face barriers to these services. For one in seven American adolescents, health insurance coverage is simply not available, and for many more it is inadequate. Within the Medicaid population, only one-third of eligible adolescents are currently covered because of funding constraints, and this proportion is unlikely to increase in the foreseeable future.[25] Health insurance for working families may not be provided by employers or, when provided, may not include their adolescent children.

Coverage of adolescents is a critical part of the debate over health care reform. As managed care spreads rapidly throughout the United States, it will be crucial to include explicit provisions for comprehensive coverage of adolescents.[26] This will be especially important to monitor, along with such matters as access, quality, and continuity of care, as states increasingly enroll their Medicaid population in managed care plans. Managed care organizations should be encouraged to contract with school-based health centers serving adolescents. Even when health coverage is available, adolescents may have inadequate information about the availability of services, or they may be concerned that confidentiality will be breached. Too often, health services are not user-friendly for adolescents. Some community health and school-based adolescent health centers have demonstrated how these barriers can be overcome.[27]

DEVELOPING APPROPRIATE HEALTH PERSONNEL AND SCHOOL-RELATED SERVICES

Currently, there is a dearth of experienced and well-trained health providers who can sensitively treat the health problems of adolescents, with special attention to continuity of care. Of equal concern is the lack of adequate preparation of the larger number of nonspecialist physicians, nurses, nutritionists, psychologists, and social workers who must work as part of a multidisciplinary team to deal effectively with the adolescents they encounter.[28]

Serious gaps must be filled in service systems for all adolescents, especially those with multiple health problems, chronic disease, or disability, such as attention deficit disorder.[29] One promising approach to filling this service gap is by establishing more school-related health facilities expressly for young adolescents, either at the school or near the school and functionally integrated with it with respect to both curriculum and accessibility. Such facilities have demonstrated their ability to deal with acute medical problems, including mental health. They have strong potential for disease prevention and health promotion.

States and communities, with help from the federal government and private funds, already have established more than six hundred school-based or school-linked health centers nationwide since 1980. Local health professionals and institutions work with the schools to provide these services. National health and education organizations have issued policy statements supporting these centers, including the American Medical Association, the Association of School Nurses, the American Academy of Pediatrics, the National Education Association, the National Association of State Boards of Education, the Society for Adolescent Medicine, the American College of Obstetrics and Gynecology, and the American Public Health Association.

In 1995, the National Assembly of School-Based Health Clinics was established. Parents also are supportive of the centers and of adolescents' use of them. The average annual cost per student of these centers is less than $200.[30]

Students use these services primarily for physical examinations, acute illness, and minor emergencies. Since students often request help with feelings of depression, loneliness, and anxiety, these centers also should provide appropriate mental health services. There is an important opportunity here; treatment of depression, for example, can prevent self-medication leading to substance abuse and addiction.

Until now, most of these centers have operated in high schools. Reproductive health care accounts for less than 20 percent of the services provided there.[31] In middle grade schools, an even lower percentage is expected. Evidence suggests that counseling can delay the initiation of sexual activity.[32] Nevertheless, some young people become sexually active during the middle grade years. Therefore, it is appropriate for school-based or school-linked centers to provide family planning information. School-based centers should be open beyond school hours, have outreach programs and trained staff, and receive community-wide support.

THE PROMISE OF HEALTHIER LIVES

The early adolescent years are increasingly the starting point of an upsurge of health-compromising behaviors that have lifelong ramifications. Although grim statistics about the health of adolescents are a continual reminder of the potentially tragic consequences of choices at this age, early adolescence presents an often overlooked opportunity for health promotion. Properly nurtured, adolescents' interest in their own developing bodies can be a potent force for building healthy lifestyles of enduring significance. The best chance to fulfill this promise lies in connecting health care professionals with schools, community organizations, families, and media.

A crucial ingredient in this formula for lifelong health is the guiding and motivating influence of caring adults. Information and skills are not sufficient to influence the behavior of adolescents unless they are willing and able to put them to use in the interests of fostering their own health. To encourage this willingness requires the protection and support of their families, friends, health professionals trained to work effectively with the adolescent age group and other adults.

Health promotion assumes that adolescents will have access to primary health care services for prevention and early intervention. Health policymakers must work with communities and families to find new ways to improve adolescents' access to health care services through stable primary care providers or through school-linked adolescent health centers that emphasize preventive services, including dental and mental health care. Schools and communities alike must become places that enhance healthy behaviors among adolescents and the people around them.

A comprehensive health-promotion strategy, therefore, requires a community-wide commitment not only from adolescents but from the full range of institutions with whom adolescents are involved. Making this commitment to young adolescents is potentially one of the most powerful means of changing health outcomes for life.

A member of the Carnegie Council on Adolescent Development, Michael I. Cohen, chair of the Department of Pediatrics at the Albert Einstein College of Medicine, served as vice chair of the advisory panel for the Office of Technology Assessment (OTA) study of adolescent health. In a presentation before the Carnegie Board of Trustees, he called attention to the highlights of the first national study on the health of American adolescents:

■ **Collection of health statistics should be informed by developmental phases within the adolescent period.** Researchers have divided the adolescent period roughly into three phases: early, middle, and late. The use of chronological age, given individual variability at a specific age during adolescence, is not a good substitute for developmental status. However, currently published data make it difficult to organize information based on these phases and on adolescence itself. For example, national data are often reported for "children below the age of eighteen" or "for youth from fifteen to twenty-four." The OTA study has focused more attention on the adolescent years, and increasingly health statistics are being reported for adolescents from ten to fourteen and from fifteen to nineteen years, as indicated in this report.

■ **Collection of health statistics should take into account important characteristics of diversity within the American adolescent population.** Data are typically reported by race and ethnicity and by gender. Since the OTA report, and reflecting changes in the U.S. population, more statistical reporting includes Hispanic-Latino, American Indian, and Asian Pacific adolescents. However, information that separates race or ethnicity from socioeconomic status is still rare.

■ **Behavioral science research is crucial to understanding the new behavior-linked morbidities of adolescence. Research on adolescent development and health must be a high national science policy priority.** Adolescents have been commonly regarded as the healthiest Americans and those in least need of health services. However, OTA's analysis suggested that one out of every five adolescents has at least one serious health problem. Increasingly, these problems are behavioral in nature, including drug abuse, accidents and injuries, homicides, suicides, sexually transmitted diseases, and premature pregnancy. Research that seeks to understand paths to healthy outcomes in adolescence and contributing risk factors—individual, familial, and social—is urgently needed for informed, effective prevention approaches.

■ **Disease prevention and health promotion are crucial during the adolescent years.** Health care agencies and professionals, using current understanding about the behaviorally based factors related to adolescent health status, must work toward achieving a better balance between treatment of illness and health promotion and disease prevention.

■ **A variety of approaches to healthy adolescent development must be tested.** Adolescents are a diverse group, and many organizations, including health agencies, can foster healthy lifestyles in this age group. As a major option, OTA sees special promise in school-related health centers, as well as community-based, comprehensive adolescent health centers.

■ **Health professionals must be prepared to work with adolescents.** While adolescent health specialists are still rare within the health professions, an even greater problem exists in preparing health professionals—nonspecialist physicians, nurses, psychologists, and social workers—to work effectively with the adolescents they encounter.

■ **Health care reform must take into account the developmental needs of adolescents.** Any reform of health care financing and provision of services must include attention to adolescents as a group with needs separate from young children.

SOURCE

U.S. Congress, Office of Technology Assessment. (1991). *Adolescent health-Volume I: Summary and policy options.* Washington, DC: U.S. Government Printing Office.

An Integrated Approach to Health Promotion

Depression, suicide, alcohol and drug use, HIV/AIDS and other sexually transmitted diseases, gun-related homicides—this is the minefield of deeply disturbing health problems American adolescents in the 1990s have to cross. For young people to grow up healthy, an integrated approach is necessary—one that takes into account individual responsibility for health as well as society's responsibility to support individuals' decisions to enhance their health.

■ **Adolescents need information.** To develop healthy habits and avoid risks, adolescents need facts. They need to know the importance of good nutrition and exercise, the harmful consequences of substance abuse, and the responsibilities of sexual involvement. Furthermore, students need the facts early. These facts should be part of the core curriculum in the higher elementary school grades and in the middle schools. Life sciences classes can teach students how their minds and bodies develop and function, what strengthens them, and what harms them.

■ **Adolescents need critical life skills.** To protect their health and expand their options, adolescents need life skills such as problem solving, planning, decision making, resisting negative influences of peers and the media, resolving conflict nonviolently, and coping with stress. Because of profound changes in our nation over the last few decades, however, it is

no longer safe to assume that the skills necessary for succeeding—or even surviving—in a complex society are being transmitted. When coupled with social support networks, such training can help adolescents make wise, informed decisions and steer clear of high-risk behavior.

■ **Adolescents need health services, including preventive health, dental, and mental health care.** Many adolescents lack access to the health services they need. One way to rectify this situation is to extend insurance coverage—both public and private—to all adolescents. Another way is to establish health centers in or near schools. Cooperative efforts among education, health, and social service groups could provide students better access to such services. Centers should offer health promotion and disease prevention education, treat or refer students suffering from injuries and acute and chronic illnesses, and arrange for treatment of dental and vision problems. To successfully serve adolescents, centers must guarantee confidentiality.

■ **Adolescents need motivation to protect their health.** Providing information, skills, and services is not enough. To protect their health, adolescents must have incentives to put what they have learned into action. The social environment can provide these incentives. Adolescents living in poverty are more at

Further Reading

Falco, M. (1992). *The making of a drug-free America: Programs that work.* New York: Times Books.

Hechinger, F. M. (1992). *Fateful choices: Healthy adolescents for the twenty-first century.* New York: Hill and Wang.

Hendee, W. R. (Ed.). (1991). *The health of adolescents: Understanding and facilitating biological, behavioral, and social development.* San Francisco: Jossey-Bass Publishers.

Lynch, B. S., & Bonnie, R. J. (Eds.). (1994). *Growing up tobacco free: Preventing nicotine addiction in children and youths.* Washington, DC: National Academy Press.

risk for engaging in unhealthy behavior because of the cultural, social, and economic constraints they face.

- **Adolescents need the support of relatives and other adults, especially educators and health providers.** Adolescents need close, ongoing contact with caring and competent people whose judgment they trust. To establish these critical relationships, educators, mentors, health professionals, and other adults who work with adolescents should receive training in adolescent development and develop the skills needed to counsel young people effectively. Primary care providers who work with diverse populations of adolescents must be culturally sensitive and able to bridge not only the generation gap but also cultural differences that may exist.

- **Adolescents need environments that foster healthy social and economic development.** Many adolescents today live in environments where problems ranging from violence to hopelessness adversely affect their health. Neighborhoods in which the adults are connected by an extensive set of expectations, obligations, and social networks are in a better position to control and supervise the activities and behavior of children and adolescents. In neighborhoods with weak social controls and monitoring, adolescents are more likely to be affected by peer group culture and may succumb to high-risk behaviors such

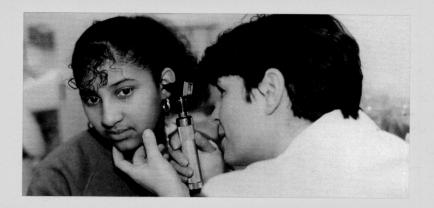

as gang involvement, alcohol and drug use, and premature sexual activity. Because the lack of employment opportunities suitable for young people compounds other problems, connecting adolescents with the world of work can have a positive effect. Mentoring programs, part-time internships during the school year and full-time internships during the summer, and apprenticeships that take a "learn-while-you-earn" approach can help adolescents feel competent and useful, improve their economic prospects, and provide a sense of a promising future.

SOURCE

Millstein, S. G., Petersen, A. C., & Nightingale, E. O. (Eds.). (1993). *Promoting the health of adolescents: New directions for the twenty-first century.* New York: Oxford University Press.

Millstein, S. G., Petersen, A. C., & Nightingale, E. O. (Eds.). (1993). *Promoting the health of adolescents: New directions for the twenty-first century.* New York: Oxford University Press.

Palfrey, J. S. (1994). *Community child health: An action plan for today.* Westport, CT: Praeger.

U.S. Congress, Office of Technology Assessment. (1991). *Adolescent health, volumes 1–3.* Washington, DC: U.S. Government Printing Office.

Wilson, M. H., Baker, S. P., Teret, S., Shock, S., & Garbarino, J. (1991). *Saving children: A guide to injury prevention.* New York: Oxford University Press.

CHAPTER EIGHT

Strengthening Communities with Adolescents

The experience of growing up in American communities has changed significantly in recent decades. For most young adolescents, the feeling of belonging to a community that offers mutual aid and a sense of common purpose, whether it is found in their families, schools, neighborhoods, houses of worship, or youth organizations, has been greatly compromised.

Each school day, America's 19 million young adolescents decide how they will spend at least five of their waking hours when they are not in school.[1] A significant number of the twelve-to-fourteen-year-olds are home alone for more than two hours each school day.[2] On weekends, holidays, and during the summer months, American youth have even greater amounts of discretionary time without adult guidance. For them, the out-of-school hours constitute a time of increased vulnerability for high-risk behavior. Those left on their own or only with peers stand a significantly greater chance of becoming involved in substance abuse, sexual activity leading to unwanted pregnancy and sexually transmitted diseases, and crime and violence than their peers who are engaged in activities with adult supervision.[3]

Young adolescents from all economic strata often find themselves alone in communities where there are few adults to turn to and no safe places to go.[4] Inadequate public transportation systems and Americans' reliance on the private car limit the ability of young adolescents to travel to activities in places such as clubs away from home or school. In some communities, the main place to meet others and socialize is in a shopping mall. Where such malls do not exist, the streets offer ample opportunities for illegal and often dangerous, violent activities.

Time spent alone is not the crucial contributor to high risk. What adolescents do during that time, where they do it, and with whom leads to either positive or negative results. The task is to turn the now-lost opportunities of the out-of-school hours into attractive, growth-promoting settings. Many youth and community organizations, in partnership with schools and corporations, are beginning to respond.

In the critical transition from childhood toward a still-distant adulthood, adolescents have a lot to learn—not only about new subjects at school but also about people, career opportunities, places beyond the neighborhood, arts, sciences, and themselves. Families help. Schools help. But increasingly they are not enough.

I'll be going to middle school next year. I'll be in the sixth grade. I come to the community center to play basketball, lift weights, have other activities and stuff. It's fun, 'cause my friends are here and it's much better than sitting at home and watching TV all day. It's like a place where I can come when I'm bored, 'cause there's always people that can help me whenever I have problems or anything. Also I've got somebody here that I can depend on. I have my friend Greg in the other room. He gives me advice, we play basketball together, and he takes me out and stuff.

TERENCE, 11

More than 17,000 national and local youth organizations now operate in the United States.[5] These youth organizations include both large national organizations and small, independent grassroots organizations not affiliated with a national structure. Some are private, nonprofit agencies whose central mission is to provide opportunities for youth, such as the Boy Scouts, 4-H Clubs, the YMCA, and YWCA. The potential of these youth organizations can be extended greatly by adult service groups, such as Rotary or Kiwanis Clubs, religious organizations, minority organizations, sports leagues, arts programs, senior citizens' groups, museums, and public-sector institutions such as libraries and parks and recreation departments.

A Carnegie Council report, *A Matter of Time: Risk and Opportunity in the Nonschool Hours*, focused attention on how youth-oriented organizations can play an urgently needed and expanded role in helping America's young people prepare for lives as responsible, inquiring, and vigorous adults. The report illustrated ways that these organizations can extend family- and school-like functions into the crucial after-school, weekend, and summer hours when neither schools nor parents are available to provide supervision. Youth organizations can connect young adolescents with reliable adults who provide social support and guidance while offering young adolescents opportunities to be of service to their communities, learn about the world of work, earn money, build a sense of worth, and make durable friendships.

A Matter of Time noted that promising programs already exist, but they reach all too few of the young people who most need their support and guidance. Some 29 percent (approximately 5.5 million) of young adolescents are not served by any of the existing 17,000 youth organizations.[6] Many programs for youth operate only an hour or two a week, which is neither intensive enough nor adequate in time to meet essential needs for healthy adolescent development. Many programs, too, are run by well-meaning adults who are untrained in dealing with young adolescents and their distinctive attributes. Membership in these groups declines precipitously as children move into adolescence. When these programs do not address requirements and interest of developing adolescents, as is often the case, the young people drift away.

Elements of Effective Youth Programs

Based on its three-year study of youth and community organizations, the Carnegie Council's Task Force on Youth Development and Community Programs identified characteristics of community programs that are responsive to the needs of young adolescents. Such programs

- Are safe and accessible to all youth. They should be located in safe, easy-to-reach settings that are open to all youth who seek them out. Programs in school facilities during the after-school hours may have an advantage of providing such an environment but must be year-round operations and open during the evenings, weekends, and vacations to avoid a dangerous vacuum. Transportation and child care are often needed if all adolescents are to have genuine access to these opportunities.

- Tailor their content and methods to the characteristics, interests, and diversity of young adolescents based on a systematic assessment of community needs and existing services. Programs should be enjoyable, culturally relevant, and linked to activities that capture adolescents' interests, such as sports and recreation, drama, business skills, the arts, life skills, and academic enhancement. Programs need to be flexible enough to respond to adolescents' requests to integrate new activities, as they are needed and reasonable, into the ongoing program.

- Work with a variety of other community organizations and governmental agencies to extend their reach to vulnerable adolescents, especially those in resource-poor neighborhoods. They should offer a wide array of services, including primary health services—substance abuse prevention, mental health, and family planning—that facilitate healthy development.

- Strengthen the preparation and the diversity of their adult leadership. Staff of youth organizations should be knowledgeable about the development of adolescents and prepared to work with them.

- Enhance the participation of young adolescents as resources to building and improving their communities. Activities should involve young people in all aspects of program development, including day-to-day planning. Young adolescents' contributions to the program and their communities should be regularly recognized and publicly rewarded. In many communities, young adolescents' desire to gain meaningful employment skills and experiences can be met through community and service programs and by career awareness and job skills classes.

- Reach out to families, schools, and other community partners to create stronger community support systems for young adolescents. They can provide linkages to schools as a way to support the academic achievement and learning of young adolescents. Such programs should encourage parental participation by creating real opportunities to become involved in the life of the school and in improving their own education and training.

- Identify their objectives and evaluate their methods and outcomes for young adolescents, staff, and community impact. Process evaluations enable staff to adapt and improve what they are doing. Outcome evaluations can provide information on near term outcomes. However, it must be recognized that important outcomes, such as employment in the legitimate workforce, may not be measurable until some years later.

- Advocate vigorously for and with youth to improve opportunities for education and health in their communities.

- Establish strong organizations with a vision of youth development, led by energetic and committed board leadership.

- Strengthen research on community organizations and youth development, giving it a higher priority in science policy than ever before because of the potential importance of these opportunities to prevent casualties in adolescence and beyond.

SOURCE

Task Force on Youth Development and Community Programs. (1992). *A matter of time: Risk and opportunity in the nonschool hours.* New York: Carnegie Corporation of New York.

Collaborating for Youth

Boys & Girls Clubs in Public Housing Projects

Low-income neighborhoods often lack safe places for young adolescents to congregate and to participate in recreational or educational activities. Meeting the needs of adolescents living in these areas is the mission of the Boys & Girls Clubs of America, a national federation of independent local clubs.

Opening their doors to all young people, ages six to eighteen, clubs offer a wide variety of activities. Grouped in six core areas, these include health and physical education, personal and educational development, citizenship and leadership development, cultural enrichment, recreation, and outdoor environmental education. Through these activities, the clubs hope to instill such values as good work habits, self-reliance, perseverance, teamwork, and consideration of others. Club programs are designed to provide girls and boys with responsible adult guidance, encouragement and support that are frequently not available at home, in school, or elsewhere in the community.

Each year, Boys & Girls Clubs serve 2 million young people. More than half of these youth come from minority groups, single-parent households, or low-income families. To reach even more young people in need, Boys & Girls Clubs launched an ambitious new initiative in 1987. At the heart of the plan was the decision to expand its efforts in public housing projects. Today, with the ongoing support of the U.S. Department of Housing and Urban Development and several key federal agencies and private foundations, 270 clubs are located in housing projects nationwide and in Puerto Rico. They are also the only national youth-serving agency with a major presence in public housing. Through this public-private collaboration, thousands of young people have a positive alternative to hopelessness and lives frequently filled with violence.

Research conducted over a three-year period in fifteen public housing projects has shown that these clubs have a positive impact on parental involvement and school performance, and their presence also encourages residents to organize and improve their community. The clubs also had positive effects on reducing drug use, juvenile crime, and the presence of crack in housing projects compared to housing projects without them. Boys & Girls Clubs in public housing are significant for two key reasons: They are responsible for bringing about many broad-based and dramatic social changes, and they provide a self-sustaining program of assistance.

When asked what they want from programs, young adolescents say they want secure and stable relationships with caring peers and adults, safe and attractive places to relax and be with their friends, and opportunities to develop life skills, contribute to their communities, and feel competent.[7] Good youth programs offer precisely what adolescents want: mentoring and coaching relationships; drop-in activities; development of social skills; safe havens; community service; and programs that nurture interests and talents, public performance, and recognition.

To expand the reach of good programs, the Council's report urged the development of innovative partnerships that can provide these organizations with financial and other resources. For example, several federal agencies provide such organizations with funds directed toward their preventive potential in areas of substance abuse and youth violence.[8] With both public and private funds, these community-based organizations can reach neglected adolescents, who are likely to benefit a great deal from opportunities to belong to a valued group. These settings present a powerful alternative to the appeal of youth gangs and other negative influences.

A Matter of Time has contributed to efforts across the country to recreate communities with youth. Urban parks and recreation groups used the report to argue for more safe, open spaces, particularly in neighborhoods of concentrated poverty.[9] Theater and arts groups cited its findings in their requests for increased support of their activities. Federal agencies pointed to the report when including after-school programs as part of a crime-prevention strategy.[10] National youth organizations turned to it for guidance in reorganizing their priorities. In several cities, including San Francisco, Chicago, and Denver, the report was the basis for examining how youth-serving agencies in both the public and private sectors could better meet the needs of adolescents in their cities.[11] All of these efforts are the hopeful signs of movement toward what John Gardner, a member of the task force that issued the report, called "reinventing community" to adapt to new social conditions.[12]

COMMUNITY ORGANIZATIONS AS A WAY OF OVERCOMING DISADVANTAGE

Young adolescents from families with very low incomes are likely to live in unsafe neighborhoods and to be unsupervised during the out-of-school hours. Already penalized by economic disadvantage and the stresses of life in their neighborhoods, they also are the least likely to have access to enriching youth programs in their neighborhoods.[13] They are at extremely high risk. They are young people whose lives hang in the balance.

Communities of color are trying to focus their institutions on encouraging young people to stay in school and pursue education in a determined way even in the face of frustration. Much can be accomplished by community-based youth organizations to support and extend the educational functions of schools. A variety of organizations and institutions can provide long-term mentors who are like parents, older siblings, and an extended family. Across the country, examples of such interventions exist.

Some programs are based in churches (such as Project SPIRIT, the initiative of the Congress of National Black Churches); some are based in community organizations (such as the Boys & Girls Clubs); others involve youth service (such as CityYouth L.A. and the Early Adolescent Helper Program); others are based in minority organizations, including the National Coalition of Hispanic Health and Human Service Organizations, National Urban League, minority fraternities and sororities, and ASPIRA.[14] National scientific associations, such as the American Association for the Advancement of Science, are working with churches and other community organizations to increase young people's interest and active involvement in the sciences. Through the Association of Science-Technology Centers, science and youth museums throughout the country are involving adolescents from low-income communities as docents and exhibition designers.

Pursuing such efforts typically requires the involvement of neighborhood residents and volunteers who know their communities well. Usually there is need for a highly competent corps of paid staff working with able and dedicated volunteers and for firm links with relevant professionals. Promising models exist, but there is no large-scale system. As worthwhile lines of innovation emerge, it is crucial to have careful evaluations so that the effects can be broadly understood. What works for whom under what conditions? Such knowledge can help in scaling up the best efforts for use where they are most needed.

Among the most powerful means of enriching young lives is to enlist their energies in improving their own communities. Young adolescents can and want to contribute to their communities, and they learn much from such engagement. Aside from experiencing the rewards of service to others, they learn skills and develop habits that will serve them well in the world of work.

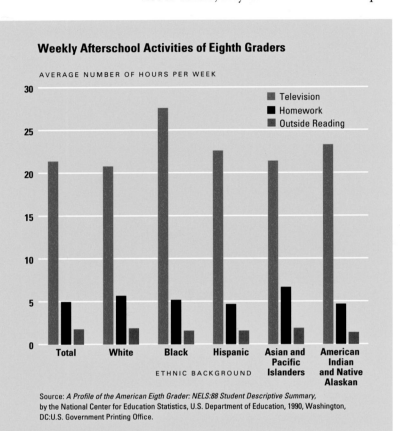

Weekly Afterschool Activities of Eighth Graders

AVERAGE NUMBER OF HOURS PER WEEK

■ Television
■ Homework
■ Outside Reading

ETHNIC BACKGROUND

Source: *A Profile of the American Eigth Grader: NELS:88 Student Descriptive Summary,*
by the National Center for Education Statistics, U.S. Department of Education, 1990, Washington,
DC:U.S. Government Printing Office.

They learn about the importance of collaborative problem solving when teams work together to achieve group objectives; about the importance of being prompt, courteous, and cooperative; and about the inevitable necessity of patience and persistence in pursuing long-term goals. Under the auspices of the American Library Association, as one example, public libraries are addressing adolescents' needs with programs that include paid employment and volunteer opportunities to work with younger children.

When programs encourage young adolescents to participate in community life as valued resources, they enable young people to become stakeholders in the community's values, traditions, and accomplishments. Adolescents with such a sense of belonging are more likely to choose positive paths to achievement. Their self-efficacy grows as they see their contributions bear fruit. Adolescents often adopt as role models the adult leaders who help them build their own futures.

To be successful, service learning programs must take into account the interests and talents of young adolescents and the ways in which they learn. Activities must be carefully planned to offer meaningful experiences with tangible results so that young adolescents feel a sense of accomplishment. Often the most successful programs are ones in which young people participate in all aspects of program development, including day-to-day planning. In addition, building pride in solid accomplishments must be part of the core of the program. Young adolescents' contributions to the program and their communities should be regularly recognized and publicly rewarded.

STRENGTHENING ADULT LEADERS IN COMMUNITY ORGANIZATIONS

The adult leaders in community organizations often are available to young people at all hours of the day, labor without adequate compensation, have limited benefits, and go unrecognized for their contributions to youth and community development. Yet they are society's frontline workers who breathe life into youth programs.

Community Service Opportunities

Community service can be a powerful tool for young adolescents to learn about important human values such as compassion, cooperation, tolerance, respect, and fairness. That is one of the reasons *Turning Points* recommends that community service be a part of middle schools' core curriculum.

Often called "service learning," community service activities can reinforce skills like problem solving and conflict resolution taught in other parts of the curriculum. In fact, the most effective programs integrate service learning into the traditional curriculum, embedding activities in the study of mathematics, science, language, art, or social studies in ways that encourage interdisciplinary integration and team teaching. Service learning can take place virtually anywhere. At school, students can serve as peer tutors, teaching assistants, or other kinds of helpers. Away from school, they can be child care volunteers or environmental workers.

CITYYOUTH, L.A.: EDUCATION AND COMMUNITY ACTION

One noteworthy example of service learning is City Youth, L.A.: Education and Community Action. Sponsored by the Constitutional Rights Foundation, the program gives teachers the training and materials to help their pupils use what they have learned in

school to identify, analyze, and address community problems. Using oral histories and other activities, the CityYouth curriculum helps teachers and students understand such community issues as health, safety, and crime and provides the skills students need to address community problems. The CityYouth curriculum also promotes respect for the racial, ethnic, and socioeconomic diversity characteristic of Los Angeles's student population. The Los Angeles Unified School District piloted the program in 1992 in four middle schools, involving about 150 students. Today the program features nine teaching teams who reach a thousand students.

EARLY ADOLESCENT HELPER PROGRAM

The Early Adolescent Helper Program is another approach to service learning. A program of the National Helpers Network, it has promoted service learning among young adolescents since 1982. With the dual goals of raising adolescents' self-esteem and improving communities with adolescents' service, the program views community service as a valuable part of adolescent education. The Helpers Network has developed two intergenerational programs. The Learning Helpers Program creates opportunities for young adolescents to assist in after-school programs for children. Learning Helpers read aloud to children, supervise their play, and teach them games. The Partners Program gives adolescents the chance to work with older people at senior centers and nursing homes. Other programs focus on environmental issues, neighborhood improvement, and tutoring. In addition to their community service, students participate in weekly seminars designed to stimulate reflection on their active involvement in community settings. Led by trained adults, these seminars use curricula developed by the Network.

Black Churches Support Youth Development Through Project SPIRIT

Since 1978, the Congress of National Black Churches (CNBC) has worked to build on and strengthen the black church's ministry by serving as an organizational umbrella for the eight major Black American religious denominations. Headquartered in Washington, D.C., CNBC represents approximately 19 million African Americans in more than 65,000 local churches.

CNBC seeks to harness the historical mission of black churches to respond not only to the spiritual but also to the economic and social needs of the black community. The organization launched its first major national demonstration effort—Project SPIRIT— in 1986. Project SPIRIT, which stands for *Strength, Perseverance, Imagination, Responsibility, Integrity,* and *Talent,* aims to instill those very qualities in African American youth, ages six to twelve. Goals of the project are to provide constructive after-school activities for young people growing up in low-income communities, to expand their network of relationships with caring adults, to support academic achievement, and to teach practical life skills. The project focuses on three target populations: Children and young adolescents, parents, and African American pastors. Project SPIRIT is currently operating in sixty-five churches in seven states—Arkansas, California, Florida, Georgia, Indiana, New York, and Minnesota—and in the District of Columbia.

The youth component revolves around daily after-school programs conducted in church facilities. Project SPIRIT generally enrolls young people who are underachievers, bored with the traditional school setting, earning low grades, and experiencing discipline problems. For three hours after every school day, they concentrate on their homework, supervised by retired or active teachers and other professionals, who are recruited into the program and trained in providing motivation and support. They then receive supplementary tutoring from workbooks and curricular materials. A portion of the afternoon is devoted to the development of African American cultural and ethnic pride and improved self-concepts as well as practical living skills through games, skits, songs, and role playing real-life experiences. Project SPIRIT also organizes Saturday programs for parents and children and provides parent education programs focused on child and adolescent development, parent-child communication, discipline, and financial management. The program has served more than two thousand children with tutorials aimed at strengthening their skills in reading, writing, and arithmetic and in building their self-esteem.

The Pastoral Counseling Training Component of Project SPIRIT provides pastors of participating churches with a fifteen-session workshop designed to help them become more effective in the care, education, and guidance of African American youth. Because this type of training is missing from most seminaries and in-service education programs for black ministers, it is a critical component of Project SPIRIT.

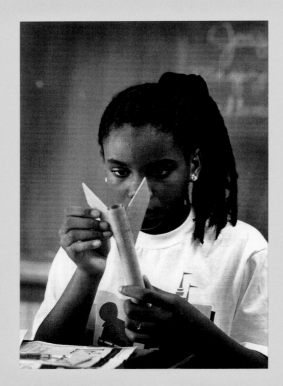

The professional development of adults, both as new and existing staff in youth organizations, is a continuing concern to the field. Different avenues to expanding opportunities for preparation for youth work, whether through postsecondary educational institutions or on the job, are now being explored by resource centers such as the Academy for Educational Development's Center for Youth Development and Policy Research.[15] These efforts are likely to enhance the effectiveness of programs experienced by young adolescents as well as increase the recognition of youth-development work as a valued service.

BUILDING YOUTH-ORIENTED COMMUNITIES

Community programs are natural partners with the other key institutions that influence young lives. These programs extend the school's responsibility for education and facilitate the transition from school to work into the out-of-school hours. They reinforce the family's responsibilities for teaching enduring values and building character during the hours when parents are not available. Ideally, these linkages will be not accidental but planned and carefully coordinated; for example, community programs can create meaningful opportunities for parents and schools to become involved in fostering and recognizing young people's accomplishments.

Adults in these key institutions can themselves cooperate to become effective advocates for youth. The voices of young adolescents rarely are heard in the corridors of policy decision making. Adolescents need powerful and well-informed adult advocates to see that their developmental requirements are met in consistent and constructive ways.

Neighborhoods and communities in today's global village often are not well organized to provide a network of support for vulnerable young adolescents. Schools, community organizations, health care institutions, and families must work together to revive for young people the experience of belonging to caring communities where all can thrive. Young adolescents, working with these organizations committed to their future, can turn their out-of-school hours into the time of their lives.

· · · · · · · · ·

Further Reading

Connell, J. P., Kubisch, A. C., Schorr, L. B., & Weiss, C. H. (Eds.). (1995). *New approaches to evaluating community initiatives: Concepts, methods and contexts.* Washington, DC: The Aspen Institute.

McLaughlin, M. W., Irby, M. A., & Langman, J. (1994). *Urban sanctuaries: Neighborhood organizations in the lives and futures of inner-city youth.* San Francisco: Jossey-Bass.

Task Force on Youth Development and Community Programs. (1992). *A matter of time: Risk and opportunity in the nonschool hours.* New York: Carnegie Corporation of New York.

Zeldin, S., & Price, L. A. (Eds.). (1995). Creating supportive communities for adolescent development: Challenges to scholars [Special issue]. *Journal of Adolescent Research, 10* (1) .

CHAPTER NINE

Redirecting the Pervasive Power of Media

The world of the adolescent cannot be understood without considering the profound influence of the mass media, especially television, but also movies and popular music. Together with the increasing penetration of cable television and video cassette recorders in American homes, these electronic conduits for programming and for the marketing of products have become strong competitors to families, schools, and community institutions in shaping young people's attitudes and values about acceptable behavior, their perceptions of what kind of society they live in, their place in that society, and their expectations of the future.

Even greater influences may emerge as the United States develops a high-speed global "information superhighway," merging signals from telephone, television, high-capacity storage media such as CD-ROM, and multimedia computers into a single medium capable of transmitting and receiving enormous amounts of information. As the potential—both positive and negative—of these new media unfold, one fact is clear: cyberspace has the potential to transform education, health care, and many of the vital aspects of life, including the experience of growing up. Already, the personal computer—the gateway to this superhighway—is becoming commonplace among more advantaged families as an interactive, home-based source of consumption, entertainment, information, and socializing.

For the near future, however, television's cheaper price, accessibility, and convenience virtually guarantee its dominion in American homes and much of the world. Adolescents unquestionably spend a great deal of time watching television: twenty-two hours per week, on average, and for some individuals as many as sixty.[1] By the time they reach age eighteen, adolescents as a group will have logged more hours in front of the television set than they will have spent in the classroom.[2] During this viewing time, the average child or adolescent will see about one thousand murders, rapes, or aggravated assaults each year.[3] Overall, adolescents from lower-income households watch more television than those from higher-income households; indeed, young people who have the poorest life chances watch more television than any adolescent group.[4]

The greatest amount of television viewing takes place among children and young adolescents. It peaks at around age twelve and declines through the later teen years in response to increasing interest in competing media, such as radio and music, and to the demands of a social life.[5] The question of what these younger adolescents are learning from these media should, therefore, be of deep concern to their families and communities.

One would have to ignore human learning capacities to suppose that media's saturation of the cultural environment has no effect on young minds. Producers of the programming and advertisements for television, radio, and other media certainly believe it is in their power to influence adolescents, who now represent a $230 billion annual market. It is because television and radio advertising are such powerful forces in shaping behavior that tobacco and alcohol commercials, except for wine and beer, have been banned from the air.

Our understanding of mass media's role in shaping adolescents' psychological development is still incomplete, but certain of its effects on the young have been established during decades of research. For example, research has shown that passive consumption of commercial television can lead to attention deficits, nonreflective thinking, irrational decision making, and confusion between external reality and packaged representations.[6] One study of the influence of entertainment television found that frequent viewing of crime shows by adolescents in grades six through twelve led them to develop an image of a mean world in which people cannot be trusted. Such an image of social reality was associated with opposition to civil liberties for persons accused of crimes.[7]

Adolescents who spend more than five hours a day sitting in front of the television set are much more likely to be obese than their counterparts who watch less than one hour.[8] The food products adolescents consume while viewing television are the same as those most advertised on the screen, notably ones high in sugar, fat, or sodium. On the other hand, in advertisements for beauty products, messages abound that in order to be accepted, girls must be thin and pretty.[9] For some girls, the ideal of thinness contributes to the development of eating disorders such as bulimia and anorexia. There is, furthermore, considerable evidence that viewing a great deal of violent content can contribute to aggressive feelings and behavior.[10] Violent content itself is not the only problem. An equally important question is whether the programming deals with conflict and violence in a responsible manner.[11] Are there consequences, such as pain? Who is the aggressor—the hero or the villain? Were other options explored before the protagonists resorted to violence? Is nonviolent resolution of conflict seriously portrayed?

There is arguably an opportunity cost in the amount of time teenagers spend in solitary, passive television watching. Young people glued to the television set are not participating in social or cultural events, excursions, or outdoor games; they are not with church, school, or musical groups. Studies also show a negative association between heavy viewing of entertainment television and academic achievement, particularly on reading tests.[12] Those who view greater amounts of television, moreover, are less likely to learn the social skills that are developed through group membership and physical activity.

Commercial television scarcely touches upon the profound social transformations that have disrupted family life and worsened economic disparities, and it rarely explores seriously the ways that ordinary families are coping. Networks consistently avoid subjects that may be of educational value to adolescents, such as contraception, because they do not consider these subjects entertaining and because they fear these subjects might offend a segment of their viewers.

Much of the attention regarding the impact of media on adolescents has focused on television. Hence, less is known about the impact of different forms of music and their lyrics, although speculation about their harmful effects is widespread.[13] Even less well understood is the cyberspace experience that a growing number of adolescents are exposed to through the use of personal computers at home or at school. The influence of what is called "virtual reality" (i.e., computers that involve the user in a multisensory experience of a simulated event) is so new that researchers can only speculate about its effects. The content readily available to adolescents through such media includes sexually explicit materials and those promoting alcohol, often disguised as infomercials. Video games tend to be exceedingly violent.

MEDIA'S CONSTRUCTIVE POTENTIAL FOR YOUTH

Despite the frequently cited negative influences of media on youth, never have the media had more potential than they do today to affect positively the lives of young adolescents. Clearly, television, video cassettes, music videos, video games, and, increasingly, computers provide interests and pleasures that are novel and attractive to teenagers and contribute to rising expectations. Even if, as now used, they are often a distraction from school and other learning opportunities, they can also be powerful tools for teaching a wide range of cognitive and social skills. They can promote compassionate understanding, nonviolent problem solving, and decent intergroup relations. They can portray human diversity while highlighting shared human experience. They can provide models of healthy development in childhood and early adolescence that increase public understanding of what it takes to raise competent youth.

Because personal computers are a growing presence in American homes, the opportunity to create programs that are educational and attractive is enormous. Health and educational professionals should seize this opportunity and collaborate with software designers to develop interactive programs that are enjoyable and educational and that actively engage participants.

THE ROLE OF REGULATION

The U.S. Federal Communications Commission requires that television networks broadcast educational children's programming as a condition of license renewal. However, the requirements do not delineate how much of this programming must be broadcast, nor do they include content standards. As part of communications deregulation in the 1980s, television stations were no longer required to air public service announcements. Today, few stations or networks make an effort to provide quality children's programming. A coalition of public interest organizations, including the Center for Media Education, is working toward requiring the networks to broadcast three hours of children's television per week.

Decades of public debate have finally led American media industries to adopt certain self-regulatory strategies that bear mention. Film and television entertainment executives have acted in recent years to avoid glamorizing alcohol, tobacco, and other drugs, although the industry's track record has not been consistent. Some local television stations have decided to limit children's exposure to advertisements for alcoholic beverages. Both the television cable networks and the video game industry have unveiled rating systems and advisories that will allow parents more control over what their children watch.[14] The Motion Picture Association of America has responded to public concern by releasing, for the first time, limited explanations of the reasons for its ratings of individual films. In addition, new technologies are being developed that could enable consumers to block out shows with specific unwanted content, such as violent programming.

Despite three decades of public debate, films, television, and certain forms of music have become increasingly more violent and often demeaning of women and other groups. In the absence of strong public clamor for change, there may be little that can be accomplished to diminish the glamorizing of violence and irresponsible sex on the screens without provoking cries of censorship from the entertainment industry. However, censorship is a matter of government action, not public pressure by private organizations. Recent surveys have shown that the public is unhappy with the increase in violent and sexually suggestive content and wants the industries involved to do more to regulate themselves.[15]

Media could do much more voluntarily to promote healthy messages and to model health-enhancing behavior in their programs and advertising. But there is also much that parents, schools, and communities can do to educate the young about the nature of this pervasive influence in their lives. As the number of homes with access to the information superhighway grows, efforts to regulate the content of electronic networks, such as the Internet, are likely to increase. By and large, this process is not likely to come from government but rather through industry self-regulation and vigorous debate in a free society with wide latitude for public criticism of dangerous practices.

INCREASING MEDIA LITERACY FOR THE INFORMATION AGE

Knowledge of media production, and especially of the ways commercial messages are shaped and used to manipulate audiences, may help protect young adolescents against strong advertising pressures to smoke, drink, have sex, or eat unhealthy foods.[16] Such knowledge also may help counter the development of social or peer norms that reinforce and maintain unhealthy behavior.

Parents should watch television shows with their children and initiate family discussions about the messages that are being communicated. Schools would do well to introduce instruction and activities that contribute to media literacy. Training in media literacy skills can be included in community and youth development programs during the out-of-school hours. Settings for television viewing that both encourage social interactions and imbue teenagers with critical habits of mind can help them become effective users of technology, restoring personal control.

Media literacy is a required part of the language arts curriculum for grades seven through twelve in Great Britain, Canada, Australia, and Spain. In contrast, teacher education, curricula, and community centers aimed at fostering media literacy in the United States are in their infancy. In many American communities, individual teachers are implementing media literacy programs in their classrooms, but district-level or statewide programs are rare. The State of New Mexico has adopted media literacy as a basic skill and pioneered a comprehensive media literacy program from kindergarten through grade twelve. North Carolina has included media literacy in both its English and information skills curricula. Efforts such as these deserve widespread consideration in schools and community organizations as an essential part of becoming a well-educated citizen.

At the threshold of the twenty-first century, media are an ever more pervasive presence in the lives of young adolescents. As heavy users of television, radio, film, and computers, adolescents are aggressively targeted as a profitable consumer market by advertisers. Their lives are saturated with entertainment and advertising. Their capacity to make sense of messages from this array of powerful sources of influence is essential to their development.

MEDIA LITERACY

Organizations such as Mediascope (discussed in this chapter) and the Center for Media Literacy have been longtime advocates of education for critical media literacy. These organizations produce books, videos, and lesson plans for parents to teach their children about the media and for teachers to create media literacy curricula for their students. The Assembly on Media Arts and the Commission on Media, both parts of the National Council of Teachers of English, have worked to make media literacy part of the national English curriculum. The efforts of these organizations have inspired the inclusion of media literacy education programs both in and out of school.

The Girl Scouts of the USA offer three badges in media literacy and communication: "Do You Get the Message?," "Basic Audiovisual Production," and "Communication Arts." To earn these badges, scouts complete activities in which they learn about computers; producing films and videotapes; analyzing advertisements in magazines, newspapers, and television; and critiquing movies and television programs. These activities include recognizing gender and racial stereotypes in the media.

Advocates for Youth is a Washington, D.C.-based organization that works to increase the opportunities for youth to make sound decisions about sexuality. Advocates for Youth created The Media Project in response to the sexual content in music videos and lyrics. Based in Los Angeles, The Media Project promotes responsible portrayals of sexuality in the entertainment media. The Project works with media professionals by sponsoring informational events and offering free consultation services to writers, producers, critics, and others. One of the project's publications, the annually produced Talking with TV, outlines the plots of television shows aimed at adolescents and suggests ways for adults to engage adolescents in honest conversation about these shows.

Girls, Inc. developed a four-part curriculum with the Center for Media Literacy called *Girls Re-Cast TV*, to teach girls to identify and counter gender biases in the media. This curriculum is designed to teach girls ages eleven to fourteen to recognize and understand stereotypes and other messages in the media. According to Isabel Stewart, executive director of Girls, Inc., "Female characters of all races, ethnicities, and abilities are still outnumbered by male characters three to one in prime time [television] and four to one in children's programs; behind the cameras, the numbers are even more discouraging." This program also offers the opportunity for girls to become involved in local media production and to learn about careers in the media.

Collectively, the various media are among the most pervasive influences in the lives of young adolescents. Media literacy education provides the opportunity for young adolescents to be active, critical consumers of media's messages. Together with families, community organizations, and schools, media-savvy adolescents may shape their own media environment in the next century.

FOSTERING COOPERATIVE CONSULTATIONS WITH THE ENTERTAINMENT INDUSTRY

Efforts to bring together professionals in media, health, education, and adolescent development on a regular basis to discuss the responsible depiction of violence and of sexual relationships have made some headway in the media entertainment industry. These efforts have led to more responsible depictions, but much more is required. A model for future cooperative efforts is the work of Mediascope and Advocates for Youth, nonprofit organizations that work with media professionals. Conferences and educational programs provide opportunities for media leaders and independent experts to cooperate in support of positive adolescent development.

As a result of such linkages, prosocial television programs such as *DeGrassi Junior High* and *In the Mix* have made serious efforts to address family conflict, emotional and physical abuse, drug abuse, AIDS, depression, and sexuality. Such successes offer some basis for hope, but the connections made must be sustained in an ongoing way for many years.

MEDIA AS PART OF COMPREHENSIVE HEALTH-PROMOTION CAMPAIGNS

Media have been successfully involved in community-wide health-promotion campaigns to prevent cardiovascular disease and to reduce the consumption of legal and illegal drugs.[17] Using a public health approach, these campaigns use television, radio, and print media, supplemented by direct interventions in community organizations and schools, to inform target audiences about risk-reducing behavior and to support individual efforts to achieve healthier lifestyles. Interventions range from the broadcast of public service announcements on radio and television to the distribution of kits on weight loss and smoking cessation.

Research and experience have shown that public service announcements alone have limited impact on behavioral change.[18] In the context of broader efforts, however, they can be valuable in directing viewers or listeners to additional sources of specific information and action. Media can be used to familiarize audiences with health-enhancing behavior, to promote products and services that foster health, and to encourage audiences to call, write, or participate in health-promotion programs.

MEETING THE CHALLENGES OF THE INFORMATION SUPERHIGHWAY

The media and entertainment industries can do much more to capitalize on their potentially positive influence on the learning, competence, and character of young adolescents. They are also one of this nation's most potent forces for improving public understanding about the requirements for positive youth development. They can join families, schools, community organizations, and health care agencies to enhance knowledge, skills, and health-promoting behavior in the young and to provide positive role models for future generations of youth who look to the media for adult images.

Connecting the Media and Adolescent Development Professionals

Mediascope, headed by Marcy Kelly, emerged from a series of seminars and meetings organized by the Carnegie Council on Adolescent Development to discuss the impact of the media on young people. Mediascope's mission is to work with media professionals in an effort to reduce violence in television, film, music, video games, and other entertainment and news presentations. The organization has sponsored many informational forums with Hollywood-based organizations such as the Writers Guild of America, the Directors Guild of America, the American Film Institute, and the Caucus for Producers, Writers, and Directors. These meetings offer creative people in the industry opportunities to confer with professionals in adolescent development, the behavioral and social sciences, health, and violence prevention. Working with a variety of entertainment industries, Mediascope is also developing voluntary guidelines and ratings that address violent content.

Kelly's approach is to persuade the entertainment industry to deal with conflict and violence in a responsible manner rather than to eliminate conflict from the screen. She believes that the media can serve as a positive influence on human behavior. As examples, she cites television's and the movies' virtual elimination of cigarette smoking on the screen and the news media's effective presentations on healthy diets and physical exercise.

The presidents of the American Psychological Association, the American Academy of Pediatrics, the American Psychiatric Association, and the Society for Adolescent Medicine have enlisted Mediascope's aid in sending a letter to 125 board chairs, chief executive officers, and other entertainment industry leaders, offering them assistance in reducing the harmful effects of media-produced violence.

For school and university classrooms, Mediascope has produced "The Kids Are Watching," a short film on children's reaction to what they see on television and in films. Typical of children's comments, Zack, a twelve-year-old participant in the program, said: "I don't remember [its name]. It was a really gross movie and there's parts in it where they wrap bodies in foil and then light it on fire, you know, and then I got a lot of scary things like that, and I get a lot of scary nightmares." The video also exposes the marketing to children of toys inspired by R-rated violent movies. It includes interviews in the Los Angeles Central Juvenile Hall, a correction facility, with adolescents who have committed violent crimes.

Mediascope is developing an ethics curriculum on violence to be used in courses that train 64,000 film students who hope to become movie makers. In 1992, the National Cable Television Association contracted with Mediascope to serve as an independent monitor to analyze and report on the level of violence on television. Mediascope, in conjunction with four universities, is monitoring the entire television industry to assess several issues, including the gratuitous use of violence, responsible scheduling, and the use of ratings and advisories. An annual report will be issued to give consumers a tool to help them make more informed choices about what they and their families watch.

Mediascope's services and resources are used by screenwriters, journalists, researchers, producers, critics, educators, media executives, members of Congress, professional associations, and students.

Promoting the Constructive Potential of the Media

An ever-expanding array of media bombard adolescents with messages that shape adolescent opinion and behavior. The power of the media can be used constructively in the lives of young people. Educators, families, and others can help enhance the constructive potential of the media in the following ways:

■ **Encourage socially responsible media programming.** Three decades of research point to a consistent, causal linkage between exposure to violence on television and aggressive behavior in children and adolescents. Violence is not the only issue, however. The media also shape adolescents' views of everything from gender, ethnic, and occupational roles to standards of beauty, family life, and sexuality. Writers, producers, directors and executives should recognize how important positive images are and work with experts on child and adolescent development so that such knowledge can be taken into account.

■ **Support public efforts to make the media more adolescent friendly.** American media basically regulate themselves when it comes to their influence on children and adolescents. Some film and television personalities, for example, try not to glamorize the use of tobacco, alcohol and other drugs. Yet much more is needed. For example, every other Western nation has stronger regulations than the United States to foster educational programming for children.

■ **Make media literacy programs a part of school curricula, of youth and community organization activities, and of family life.** Adolescents absorb a very large number of media messages every day, yet many lack the skill to analyze and evaluate those messages critically. Designed to help young people identify the media's underlying assumptions about the world, training in media literacy should cover the whole spectrum of contemporary media—including newspapers, magazines, radio, television, videos, music, computer programs, and electronic games.

■ **Use the media for comprehensive health promotion campaigns.** Successfully influencing young people's attitudes and behaviors requires a consistent message from all the social institutions that touch young people's lives. Families, schools, health care agencies, community organizations, and the media must all work together to promote messages that encourage healthy behavior. Community-wide campaigns using public service announcements in the television, radio, and print media have successfully promoted smoking cessation and physical fitness among adolescents. The entertainment industry has particular power when it comes to influencing behavior; film makers should be persuaded to depict health-enhancing behavior on the big screen.

■ **Expand opportunities to include young people's views in the media and to involve them in media production.** Media should increase the number of young voices in their publications and programs through the publication and broadcast of editorial opinions, news stories, and videos written or produced by young adolescents. Some schools have shown that this can be a useful part of education.

The emergence of a new digital electronic world via the information superhighway provides unprecedented opportunities to shape policies and practices to ensure that all children and adolescents have excellent opportunities in the next century. On-line computer and cable services already are becoming highly commercialized, and efforts to assure equitable access to information technology by all young people will be essential in our democratic society.[19] Widespread public education about the positive potential and the negative consequences of leading-edge communications technologies must be a high priority.

■ ■ ■ ■ ■ ■ ■

Further Reading

Aufderheide, P. (1992). *Media literacy: A report of the national leadership conference on media literacy.* Washington, DC: The Aspen Institute.

Christenson, P. G., & Roberts, D. F. (1990). *Popular music in early adolescence.* Washington, DC: Carnegie Council on Adolescent Development.

Flora, J. A. (1990). *Strategies for enhancing adolescents' health through music media.* Washington, DC: Carnegie Council on Adolescent Development.

Minow, N. N., & LaMay, C. L. (1995). *Abandoned in the wasteland: Children, television, and the first amendment.* New York: Hill and Wang.

Strasburger, V. C. (1995). *Adolescents and the media: Medical and psychological implications.* Newbury Park, CA: Sage Publications.

Looking to the Future:
Sustaining the Council's Perspective

DAVID A. HAMBURG

About a decade has passed since I proposed to the board and staff of Carnegie Corporation that we establish a broad-based body to consider the problems of adolescent development. This report draws that effort to a close. It is appropriate to reflect briefly on some ways in which the main thrust of the Carnegie Council's work might be carried forward in the years and even decades ahead. A long-term view is essential because we are necessarily considering difficult, indeed fundamental, changes in modern society to improve the life chances of young people.

First, let me express my heartfelt gratitude to the members of the Carnegie Council on Adolescent Development; to its executive director, Ruby Takanishi; and to the members of the staff working group and Council staff. These wonderful people are noted in the acknowledgments, and they deserve far more recognition than this report gives them. They are authentic leaders of diverse sectors and have contributed in many ways to the Council's accomplishments.

Let us keep in mind the essence of what the Council has done and why its work is likely to matter for a long time. At the outset, we made a strategic decision to focus squarely on early adolescence (ages ten to fourteen), a phase of life that is crucially formative for the entire life span and that has been badly neglected throughout most of the world.[1]

Early adolescence is a time of biological transformation and social transition, characterized by exploratory behavior, including risky behavior that has lifelong consequences. Many dangerous patterns commonly emerge during these years. Initially, adolescents explore these new possibilities tentatively with the experimental attitude that is typical of adolescence. Before damaging behavior is firmly established, therefore, there is a unique opportunity to prevent lifelong casualties.

Today's adolescents have grown up in a situation rather different from that of their parents and remarkably different from that of their grandparents. The technological world we take for granted—saturated with airplanes, telephones, radios, movies, television, computers, fax machines, compact discs and video cassettes—was much simpler a few decades ago. The technological changes linked to economic opportunities have had a huge impact on communities and on families. These changes, in turn, have had powerful effects on children and young people.

Dramatic changes also have occurred in the structure and function of American families in just a few decades. Although some of these changes represent new opportunities and bring tangible benefits, others involve serious jeopardy to the well-being of children and adolescents. The latter are common and serious enough to constitute a major challenge for the entire society.

In light of the new social conditions that have a strong impact on the experience of growing up, we must find different ways to meet the essential requirements for effective child and adolescent development—not only through the family but also through a set of pivotal institutions that have significant influence on the ultimate results. This report describes ways in which these institutions, starting with the family, can do what needs to be done in a world still relentlessly in transformation.

Let us look at what the Council actually did, so that we can consider whether certain functions ought to be continued in future years, and if so, by whom. The Carnegie Council on Adolescent Development, composed of leaders from various sectors of American society, drew together the most reliable information about adolescent development, including health, education, and the social environment. It tackled serious adolescent problems by seeking preventive interventions based, to the extent possible, on systematic research and also on careful assessment of creative innovations. Thus, best practices were identified and their improvement sought in an ongoing way through research and development.

Efforts in this field have long been plagued by professional divisions among health, education, and social service systems and by the lack of communication among people engaged in each of the individual problem domains. Similarly, there is a gap between scholars and those who run programs for young people. The result is that scholars are deprived of the direct experience of practitioners, while innovative approaches go unevaluated and their potential utility for other settings remains unknown. Consequently, many local organizations continue to pursue approaches that are plausible but lack evidence of effectiveness. Finally, there is a gap between all these people and the general public, especially parents, who in dealing with their adolescent offspring lack the kind of guidance that is widely available to them concerning younger children.

There has been no bright spotlight on adolescent development in the policy arena, no broadly integrative center for taking stock of existing approaches and stimulating new ones, no one institution where the different sectors of American society come together to pool their efforts in this field. To fill this gap, the Council established three main objectives: (1) to synthesize existing reliable information and make it widely available in intelligible form; (2) to extend this information beyond its present limits by stimulating crucial lines of research and innovation; and (3) to use reliable information more effectively by connecting the research arena with practitioners, policy makers, and the public.

Toward these ends, the Council stimulated diverse activities: studies; task forces; publications; local, national, and international meetings; working models; cooperative efforts among grant-making agencies; and linkage of independent experts with policy makers and the public.

The Council is part of Carnegie Corporation's integrated, life span strategy from conception through the adolescent years, a strategy that aims to foster every child's chance for productive adult life. A 1994 Corporation report, *Starting Points*, focused on the prenatal period through age three[2]; the Council's work highlighted early adolescence from ten to fourteen years of age. In 1996, the Corporation's Task Force on Learning in the Primary Grades will bridge the gap between ages three to ten with its recommendations for education and healthy development during the middle childhood years. A common thread woven through all of these activities is meeting the developmental needs of children and adolescents through potentially supportive institutions such as families, schools, health agencies, community organizations, and the media.

This major Corporation effort will continue in the years ahead. The main lesson learned from the Council's experience is the importance of serious, careful examination of the facts, nonpartisan analyses, broad dissemination with involvement of key sectors, and sustained commitment over a period of years.

Are there elements of the Council's work that should be continued by others in the years ahead? Presumably, some of this work will go on in ways that we cannot now foresee. The reports of the Council, including this one, are widely available and may well have continuing repercussions. They form a set of to-whom-it-may-concern messages, which should be of particular interest to the pivotal institutions and may set in motion efforts to strengthen these institutions.

WHAT BUSINESS AND GOVERNMENT CAN DO

The Council's findings and recommendations challenge other powerful institutions that can be singularly helpful—business and government, for example. Moreover, this final report and some of the Council's earlier reports connect with an informed, concerned public that can help the pivotal institutions do their jobs better.[3]

The business community can help schools and community organizations for youth in several ways: directly, by providing money, people, or both to implement recommendations made in this report;[4] indirectly, by using its considerable influence through community leadership on behalf of youth and through its impact on government at all levels. In addition, it can make its own policies and practices as family friendly as possible.[5] Another way that business can have a powerful influence is by choosing not to support violent or sexual shows with its advertising dollars. A focal point in the business community for youth development studies also could be exceedingly helpful. The work of the Committee for Economic Development on younger children and on the modern workforce provides a useful model.[6]

There is a growing consensus in the business and scientific communities that it is urgent to improve education in order for the United States to be able to compete effectively in a world economy being transformed by technological advances. If so, what is the federal role?

The role of the federal government in protecting the health of the American people is a large one, ranging from the biomedical and behavioral research of the National Institutes of Health, to the health services of Medicare and Medicaid, to the disease prevention activities of the Centers for Disease Control and Prevention. A modest but highly significant portion of these federal expenditures focuses on children and youth. Early adolescence, crucial as it is for lifelong health, has been neglected historically in federal efforts but has recently gained some attention.

One direct outgrowth of the Council's work, made possible by its Congressional members and especially the leadership of Senator Daniel K. Inouye, is the creation of an Office of Adolescent Health in the U.S. Department of Health and Human Services.[7]

When it comes to education, the federal role has traditionally been small. This fact changed under the impetus of World War II, again with Sputnik, then with the civil rights movement, and now is being reconsidered in light of the drastic, technology-driven changes in the world economy. Somehow, the powerful institutions of American society, such as federal and state governments and the business community, must address education issues of immense practical significance. These issues include

- The national interest in promoting economic vitality and growth; hence, the need for a work force with education adequate to the sophistication of contemporary and future technology.[8]

- A workforce composed increasingly of the children of immigrants, poor families, and minorities and the weak performance of the educational system in working with these groups.

- Disappointing results for students generally in such areas as mathematics, science, and problem-solving skills.

- Ineffective school structures characterized by rigid and extensive regulations, compartmentalization, and top-down management; hence, the need for leadership in judicious deregulation and for strengthening the teaching profession, which is central to the enterprise.[9]

- The growing need—far exceeding previous requirements—to build the understanding of science and technology throughout the educational system to prepare children and youth for a technically based economy and for intelligent participation as citizens in a world full of complex issues.[10]

Serious analytical work and thoughtful national discussion is needed to sort out priorities for federal and state action. State education policies have neglected adolescence. If there is indeed a crisis in education and if education is crucial for the future of our economy and democratic institutions, then we have to determine what must be done and who can do what. In our pluralistic and creative way, we surely can sort out sensible guidelines for state and federal action as well as constructive roles for other sectors. This activity should not be highly partisan, bitterly ideological, or narrow in scope. It should address realistically the problems our young people face and should formulate practical options. It should recognize the gravity of these problems and the fact that potentially valuable opportunities do indeed exist to tackle them and that all sectors, public and private, must find ways to contribute in an open-minded spirit, looking to the future of our country.

WHAT UNIVERSITIES, SCIENTIFIC INSTITUTIONS, AND PROFESSIONAL ORGANIZATIONS CAN DO

Universities, scientific institutions, and professional organizations might well pursue specific functions performed by the Council, illuminating the problems and opportunities of adolescent development, getting the facts straight, fostering objective analysis, and recognizing the implications for practice, policy, and social action. Let us briefly consider a few examples.

America's universities are recognized throughout the world as outstanding institutions of truly global significance in education and research. The attributes that have earned such respect include: high standards of science and scholarship; free and open inquiry; objective methods of assessing information and ideas; respect for diversity in people and subject matter; serious attention to opportunities for young people; broad scope of coverage of subject matter on an in-depth basis; a premium on the advancement of knowledge; and a sense of social responsibility.

These strengths can be brought to bear on child and adolescent development—a fundamental subject if there ever was one. Universities could vigorously stimulate interdisciplinary research and education on these topics; publish periodic syntheses of knowledge—not only for technical-professional audiences but also for a broader educated public; actively undertake education beyond the campus in view of the pervasive interest in these problems; link independent experts with policy makers in government, with business leaders, with responsible media or with all.

Universities and scientific academies can mobilize a wide range of talent to address great issues in a sustained and effective way. They can get the complex facts straight and clarify the most promising options in a way that is credible and intelligible to nonspecialists. Such efforts can be helpful to open-minded policy makers and also can contribute to the education of a well- informed public.

To deal effectively with real-world problems requires novel conjunctions of knowledge and talent. Many facets of a complex problem must be taken into account. The great problems do not come in packages that fit the traditional disciplines or professions, however excellent they may be. Organizations such as universities and scientific academies can make a greater contribution than they have in the past if they can organize effectively to share information, ideas, and technical abilities widely across traditional barriers of disciplines. The opportunity is clear in this field where biological, psychological, and social factors interact in shaping adolescent development.

There is an ongoing need to clarify gaps in knowledge, priorities, and scientific opportunities for research—both on fundamental aspects of adolescent development and on the utility of various interventions intended to prevent damage. From 1990 to 1994, the Council conducted annual symposia on research opportunities in adolescence.[11] The first symposium dealt with basic developmental processes during adolescence and with the influence of various institutions on that development. The second examined research gaps and scientific opportunities for improving the education and health of adolescents. The third addressed concepts of and approaches to health promotion in adolescence. The fourth focused on relations among ethnic groups during childhood and adolescence.

These symposia were remarkably well attended by leaders of both public and private grant-making organizations, including the National Institutes of Health, the National Science Foundation, and private foundations. They covered a broad spectrum of biomedical, behavioral, and social science research and have a distinguished track record of accomplishment in many fields. The Council's symposia evidently had a stimulating effect on their commitment to research in adolescent development. For example, there appeared to be substantial recognition that research in this field constitutes a great frontier for public health, because even modest gains in meeting the essential requirements for healthy adolescent development are likely to be projected through the life span. Such gains for a significant portion of the population would produce for the public a net benefit of considerable importance. The experience with these research symposia suggests that similar efforts undertaken by scientific organizations such as the National Academy of Sciences could do much to foster intellectual vitality and sustained commitment to research on adolescence, including the main factors that influence learning and healthy development.

Professional organizations are composed of large numbers of respected and dedicated people who can have a strong impact on adolescent development. There have been encouraging signs of interest by these organizations in recent years, facilitated by the Council's work and in some cases by grants from Carnegie Corporation. For example, the National Board for Professional Teaching Standards has given a high priority to developing sophisticated assessment procedures for teachers who work in early adolescent education. This effort is likely to inspire teachers and could in due course greatly strengthen the capability of middle grade schools.[12] Similarly, the American Medical Association (AMA) undertook a remarkable initiative on adolescent health, one that has been sustained over a period of years.[13] The AMA's effort has produced important publications, one of which is summarized in this report. It has held a variety of meetings and has had a constructive effect not only on medicine but also to some extent on other health professions.

It is not difficult to imagine other efforts similar to these two. For instance, educational organizations could pursue the recommendations of *Turning Points* on a systematic basis and also foster links between schools and other useful entities: community organizations, along the lines suggested by *A Matter of Time*; organizations of the health sector, to pursue the recommendations of the health chapter; and scientific organizations, to strengthen science education. In the same vein, other health professional organizations could follow up on the American Medical Association's initiative, especially to build links with middle grade schools but also to build links with the media for health promotion. Such activities could provide vital foci of innovation in many communities.[14]

MOBILIZING COMMUNITIES FOR YOUTH

At a Carnegie Corporation meeting in 1994, John Gardner discussed American renewal and made this suggestion:

Let us persuade our fellow Americans that they—as citizens— have to move with energy and discipline to solve their problems, bringing to bear all the dynamism that the American people are capable of when they put their hearts into something. Let us tell people that there is hope. Let us get the word out about the good grass-roots problem solving that is going on. Let us tell them that there is hard, hard work ahead if we are to put our country back on a good track—and there is a role for everyone. Let us tell them that there are innumerable ways in which they can help build community, help the young and the old, help reduce the tensions that lead to conflict.[15]

In this spirit, a number of attractive possibilities arise. If there is a concerted effort across different sectors, it would be possible to mobilize communities to support adolescents and their families. With a combination of informed leadership and vigorous grass-roots organizing, it would be possible to focus the attention of most communities on the needs of adolescents and their families by initiating a community-based strategic planning process. We could create community councils for youth, with active participation of relevant professionals, business and media leaders, local organizations, and adolescents themselves. Such councils would carefully assess local needs, formulate useful interventions, and inform the entire community about problems and opportunities. Participation of local media would be important.

Governments at local, state, and federal levels could remove the obstacles faced by communities in their attempts to provide more effective services and otherwise open up opportunities for healthy, constructive adolescent development. Mechanisms could be established at the state level to formulate comprehensive policy and program plans that focus on the second decade of life and to help communities translate these plans into action.

As a practical matter, it will be necessary to achieve cooperation among several institutions in a particular community. The mix might well differ from one community to another. Schools, universities, clinics, social service agencies, the media, churches, business, community organizations, government at various levels, and professional organizations—all could be highly constructive in cooperative efforts for youth development.

Any such combination of institutions could serve several valuable functions. They could

- Clarify the nature of child and adolescent problems

- Stimulate interest and hope in the possibility of useful interventions

- Help families meet their fundamental responsibilities

- Facilitate the delivery of appropriate services

- Provide resources—not only money but also people, organization, and technical skills

- Organize a steady flow of reliable and up-to-date information about what works and for whom in fostering adolescent development

The past decade has seen the rapid growth of links between schools and the nation's colleges and universities, business organizations, and a great variety of community organizations. Such partnerships are situations of mutual benefit for the schools and the cooperating organizations, but they are not sufficiently extensive. They do show what can be done by pooling strengths.

Crucial components exist all across the country and in other nations as well. We can learn how to put these components together in ways that provide adolescents with the full range of developmental opportunities permitted by today's knowledge and emerging research findings.

A variety of innovations involving cooperation among various sectors of American society have arisen in recent years to address adolescent needs in education, health, and the social environment. Here are a few examples at different levels of organization: state, county, and city.

WHAT STATES CAN DO

Turning Points marked the beginning of Carnegie Corporation's effort to stimulate nationwide reform of American middle grade schools. The report offered a plan of action for transforming middle grade schools into learning environments suited to the needs of young adolescents and equal to the challenges of a rapidly changing world. To date, approximately 86,000 copies of the full report and 185,000 copies of the abridged version have been distributed.

In 1990, Carnegie Corporation initiated the Middle Grade School State Policy Initiative (MGSSPI), a program of grants to states to stimulate statewide changes in middle grade educational policy and practice. The MGSSPI is a useful example of what states can accomplish in cooperation with the private sector. The states' work to reform middle grade education has produced impressive results. Fifteen states currently receiving Corporation support are actively implementing comprehensive middle grade policies reflecting *Turning Points*. Schools in several states report impressive gains in student achievement over the past few years. The states have employed a variety of sophisticated methods to assist schools. The Corporation has funded two research studies that together serve as an evaluation of the MGSSPI, and the results of the evaluation are encouraging. In general, the more extensive the implementation, the better the results. State policies and practices can indeed make a constructive difference.

WHAT COUNTIES CAN DO

A county initiative in North Carolina, called Smart Start, rallies local energy on behalf of children.[16] Although Smart Start does not deal with adolescents, it demonstrates how such an effort can be effectively organized at the county level. It aims to provide high-quality child care, health care, and other critical services to every child in the state under the age of six. Guided by the North Carolina Partnership for Children, a nonprofit, nonpartisan organization established by the legislature, Smart Start allocates money to selected counties that have achieved a mandatory first step: bringing together a broad range of individuals in the interest of children.

Collaboration is key. The bylaws of the Partnership designate nineteen community members who must serve on local boards, including the superintendent of schools, two business leaders, two members of low-income families with preschool children, the president of a local community college, one representative of the religious community, a Head Start representative, and the director of the local health department. The local partnerships have the freedom to create plans that will serve the specific needs of their community. State investment has been substantial and the level of cooperation across sectors has been impressive. Similar efforts could be made on behalf of youth, organized by counties in collaboration with state governments and the private sector.

Effective antidrug coalitions draw on the strength of powerful local businesses, churches, universities, and foundations. Kansas City's Metropolitan Task Force on Alcohol and Drug Abuse builds on the success of its comprehensive community prevention program, which engages the city's schools, media, and civic leadership. This program, called STAR, provides financial and technical support for the task force.[17] STAR works with local residents to discourage drinking and drug use among young people; it conducts training sessions for parents, community leaders, and concerned citizens. These groups explore their own attitudes toward drugs and study ways in which individuals can make a contribution to preventing substance abuse in the community.

Community coalitions channel citizens' concerns into efforts that require active participation, connecting people to one another and to their communities in new ways. These activities generate intense energy as coalition members discover they can have an impact on important and difficult problems. This sense of mission and efficacy is critically important in overcoming the hopelessness and apathy that often inhibit communities.

The Kansas City coalition shows the value of strong participation by a critical mass of local leadership—a foundation, academic and business organizations, and civic and religious groups. Although involvement of local governments is useful, these coalitions are largely volunteer efforts. They depend on the commitment of their members and the leadership of a few highly dedicated individuals. Sustaining that commitment over years is a crucial task. Coalitions often respond by creating a small professional staff to organize long-term efforts. Fundamentally, these efforts must engage different sectors of the community in a common cause, led largely by respected volunteers who care deeply about the future of their community. What has happened in Kansas City suggests the potential of community coalitions for youth.

A more recent effort has been undertaken in Chicago, where in 1993 the mayor appointed a group of twenty community, corporate, academic, and civic leaders and young people to the Mayor's Youth Development Task Force. Over a year's time, the task force gathered information from diverse perspectives: community organizations, religious leaders, corporate leaders, youth experts, and young people themselves. The task force decided to concentrate on the opportunities available to school-age children during nonschool hours in the spirit of the Council's report, *A Matter of Time*.

The task force called for rewriting the social contract with youth, spelling out clear roles and responsibilities for various sectors: community groups and religious organizations; businesses and foundations; local, state, and federal agencies; parents; and young people themselves. In its "Chicago for Youth" report, the task force proposed "Blueprints for Change."[18] The report was followed by the creation of a Chicago for Youth office to promote coordinated neighborhood efforts on behalf of youth and families. Funds were provided to create a strong infrastructure for youth development. Ongoing support and commitment by city government, business, and community organizations will be critical to the success of this citywide youth development approach.

These illustrations are merely suggestive of what might be done. Similar efforts have recently been undertaken in different parts of the United States and in other countries as well. Such innovations require monitoring, assessment, learning from experience, and upgrading in the years to come. Participants in these efforts can profit from the Carnegie Council's experience of intersectoral collaboration for youth. New Council-like bodies may spring up to stimulate and guide such efforts.

WHAT INTERNATIONAL ORGANIZATIONS CAN DO

The Council's work has elicited interest in a variety of countries. The Council has cooperated with international organizations to create forums in which leaders from many fields could focus on early adolescence, clarifying the urgency of the problems, the likelihood of exacerbation in the midst of drastic ongoing social and economic changes that powerfully affect families and communities, and opportunities for fostering healthy adolescent development and preventing damage.[19] International organizations involved have included the Johann Jacobs Foundation,[20] the World Health Organization, and UNICEF.

The distribution of this report, additional grants made by Carnegie, and ongoing activities of the Council members and staff will continue to have stimulating effects on many people in many places. As the importance of adolescence is increasingly understood, many people will collect new data, see new opportunities, and have better ideas. Perhaps the most significant contribution of the Council in the long run will be to set in motion an ongoing, far-flung process of building on its work and of moving far beyond it.

INVESTING IN OUR FUTURE

The United States is suffering heavy casualties during childhood and adolescence— in educational failure, poor health, and very high-risk behavior. Generally, these casualty rates are considerably higher than those of other technically advanced democracies, although similar problems exist in many countries. Given the heavy and growing burdens of disease, disability, ignorance, incompetence, hatred, and violence, the Council has mobilized a wide range of research evidence and carefully assessed innovations to determine what could be done to reduce the casualties and thereby improve the whole society. In this report, we describe and illustrate a substantial set of experiences, opportunities, and services that could make a large difference in the lives of today's youth—changing the odds favorably for a healthy and productive adult life.

To do so, we have had to make judicious use of existing evidence while wishing that a more extensive base of scientific evidence had been available. Clearly, the low priority in science policy for research on adolescent development has been a costly mistake. If the nation had given this work a priority commensurate with the gravity of the problems and the scope of the opportunities inherent in adolescent development, we could stand on firmer ground and reach higher in our aspirations.

Still, there is no reason to let the perfect become the enemy of the good. The central question is whether we can do better than we are doing now. The social costs of severely damaging conditions that shatter lives in adolescence are terrible not only in their impact on individuals but also in effects that damage the entire society—the costs of disease and disability, ignorance and incompetence, crime and violence, alienation and hatred. These distorted lives are like a virus that knows no boundaries, that cannot be contained unless prevented in the first place. Looking back over the range of evidence and experience presented in this report, there is abundant reason to believe that we can do better to provide conditions in which adolescents can grow up healthy and vigorous, inquiring and problem solving, decent and constructive.

What will it cost? A constructive sequence of developmental opportunities based on scientific evidence, professional experience, and democratic, humane values will indeed require substantial investment by parents and many others. The first and most crucial investment goes beyond economics: it deals with decent human relationships that are the essence of human adaptability. This profound investment calls for adults to give personal attention, energy, and care to children and adolescents to provide dependable attachment, protection, guidance, stimulation, nurturance, and ways of coping with adversity. To a large extent, these are family investments, both personal and economic. But it takes a social support system, a village, a community to raise children effectively and to successfully foster the adolescent's transition from childhood to adulthood. So there will necessarily be expenditures by institutions and individuals beyond the family if we are to provide good life chances for all our youth.

The expenditures required for optimal child and adolescent development are *not* all added expenses but can be achieved to a considerable extent by wiser use of existing funds. Large amounts of money are now spent for these purposes. Much of this current spending could result in improved outcomes if redirected by the approaches described in this report. For example, improving poorly functioning school systems by reducing inflated administrative structures often would cost less than we are now spending. Some new investment certainly will be required, the cost of which must largely be determined on a case-by-case, place-by-place basis. Yet the *total* economic and social costs associated with present youth-related casualties probably could be greatly reduced. These costs have many facets: economic inefficiency, loss of productivity, lack of skill, high health care costs, growing prison costs, a badly ripped social fabric, and a great deal of human suffering. One way or another, we pay heavily. Preventing the damage now occurring would have a powerful social and economic impact.

These vital investments in prevention have to be viewed as a responsibility of the *entire* society. It is the task not only of the federal government but also of other levels of government; not only of business but also of labor; not only of the public sector but also of the private sector, both nonprofit and for profit. We are all in this great leaking boat together.

Wise investment in human and social capital is the most fundamental and productive investment any society can make. The vitality of any society and the prospects for its future depend in the long run on the quality of its people, on their knowledge, skill, and opportunities, as well as on the decency of their human and social relations.

In an era when there is much well-founded concern about losing a vital sense of community, these initiatives on behalf of all our children can have profound collateral benefits of building solidarity, mutual aid, civility, and a reasonable basis for hope. What can bring us together better than our children? If there is any mission more important, I wonder what it could be.

CHAPTER ONE

Early Adolescence: The Great Transition

1. Hamburg, D. A. (1986). *Preparing for life: The critical transition of adolescence.* Presidential Essay. New York: Carnegie Corporation of New York.

2. Werner, E. E., & Smith, R.S. (1992). *Overcoming the odds: High-risk children from birth to adulthood.* Ithaca, NY: Cornell University Press.

3. Dryfoos, J. G. (1990). *Adolescents at risk: Prevalence and prevention.* New York: Oxford University Press.

4. Hamburg, D. A. (1989). *Early adolescence: A critical time for interventions in education and health.* Presidential Essay. New York: Carnegie Corporation of New York.

5. Lerner, R. M. (Ed.). (1993). *Early adolescence: Perspectives on research, policy, and intervention.* Hillsdale, NJ: Lawrence Erlbaum Associates, Inc.

6. Elliott, D. S. (1993). Health-enhancing and health-compromising lifestyles. In S. G. Millstein, A. C. Petersen, & E. O. Nightingale (Eds.), *Promoting the health of adolescents: New directions for the twenty-first century* (pp. 119–145). New York: Oxford University Press.

   Jessor, R., & Jessor, S. L. (1977). *Problem behavior and psychosocial development: A longitudinal study of youth.* New York: Academic Press.

7. Dryfoos, 1990.

8. Carnegie Corporation has addressed the needs of very young children in its 1994 report *Starting points: Meeting the needs of our youngest children.* This report focuses on the first three years of life. A Carnegie Task Force on Learning in the Primary Grades is currently synthesizing research and best practice to assure that all children in early childhood programs and elementary schools across the nation will be well educated.

9. The U.S. Congress Office of Technology Assessment report was published in three volumes by the U.S. Government Printing Office in 1991: Volume I, *Summary and policy options;* Volume II, *Background and the effectiveness of selected prevention and treatment services;* and Volume III, *Crosscutting issues in the delivery of health and related services.*

10. Hamburg, D. A. (1992). *Today's children: Creating a future for a generation in crisis.* New York: Times Books.

11. Elliott, 1993.

12. Dryfoos, 1990; Werner & Smith, 1992.

CHAPTER TWO

Growing Up in Early Adolescence: An Emerging View

1. Feldman, S. S., & Elliott, G. R. (Eds.). (1990). *At the threshold: The developing adolescent.* Cambridge, MA: Harvard University Press.

   Lerner, R. M. (Ed.). (1993). *Early adolescence: Perspectives on research, policy, and intervention.* Hillsdale, NJ: Lawrence Erlbaum Associates, Inc.

2. Werner, E. E., & Smith, R. S. (1992). *Overcoming the odds: High-risk children from birth to adulthood.* Ithaca, NY: Cornell University Press.

3. Haggerty, R. J., Sherrod, L. R., Garmezy, N., & Rutter, M. (1994). *Stress, risk, and resilience in children and adolescents: Process, mechanisms, and interventions.* New York: Cambridge University Press.

   Montemayor, R., Adams, G. R., & Gullotta, T. P. (Eds.). (1990). *From childhood to adolescence: A transitional period?* Newbury Park, CA: Sage.

4. Petersen, A. C., & Leffert, N. (1994). What is special about adolescence? In M. Rutter (Ed.), *Psychosocial disturbances in young people: Challenges for prevention* (pp. 3–36). New York: Cambridge University Press.

5. Ibid.

6. Nolen-Hoeksema, S., & Girgus, J. S. (1994). The emergence of gender differences in depression during adolescence. *Psychological Bulletin, 115,* 424–443.

7. Paikoff, R. L., & Brooks-Gunn, J. (1990). Physiological processes: What role do they play during the transition to adolescence? In R. Montemayor, G. R. Adams, & T. P. Gullotta (Eds.), *From childhood to adolescence: A transitional period?* (pp. 63–81). Newbury Park, CA: Sage.

8. Brown, B. B. (1990). Peer groups and peer cultures. In S.S. Feldman & G. R. Elliott (Eds.), *At the threshold: The developing adolescent* (pp. 171–196). Cambridge, MA: Harvard University Press.

   Savin-Williams, R. C., & Berndt, T. J. (1990). Friendship and peer relations. In S.S. Feldman & G. R. Elliott (Eds.), *At the threshold: The developing adolescent* (pp. 277-307). Cambridge, MA: Harvard University Press.

9. Who's Who among American High School Students. (1995). *A portrait of a generation: 25 years of teen behavior and attitudes.* Lake Forest, IL: Educational Communications, Inc.

   Louis Harris and Associates, Inc. (1989). *Girl Scouts survey on the beliefs and moral values of America's children.* New York: Girl Scouts of the United States of America.

10. Steinberg, L. (1990). Autonomy, conflict, and harmony in the family relationship. In S. S. Feldman & G. R. Elliott (Eds.), *At the threshold: The developing adolescent* (pp. 255-276). Cambridge, MA: Harvard University Press.

11. Brown, 1990.

12. Keating, D. P. (1990). Adolescent thinking. In S. S. Feldman & G. R. Elliott (Eds.), *At the threshold: The developing adolescent* (pp. 54–92). Cambridge, MA: Harvard University Press.

    Fischhoff, B. (1992). Risk taking: A developmental perspective. In J. F. Yates (Ed.), *Risk-Taking Behavior.* New York: John Wiley & Sons, Ltd.

    Gittler, J., Quigley-Rick, M., & Saks, M. J. (1990). *Adolescent health care decision making: The law and public policy.* Washington, DC: Carnegie Council on Adolescent Development.

13. Millstein, S. G. (1993). A view of health from the adolescent's perspective. In S. G. Millstein, A. C. Petersen, & E. O. Nightingale (Eds.), *Promoting the health of adolescents: New directions for the twenty-first century* (pp. 97–118). New York: Oxford University Press.

CHAPTER THREE

**Old Biology in New Circumstances:
The Changing Adolescent Experience**

1. Hernandez, D. (1993). *America's children: Resources from family, government, and the economy.* New York: Russell Sage Foundation.

2. Ibid.

3. Goldstein, N. (1993, January). *Are changes in work and family harming children?* Background paper prepared for the Task Force on Meeting the Needs of Young Children, Carnegie Corporation of New York.

4. U.S. Department of Education, Office of Educational Research and Improvement, National Center for Education Statistics. (1990). *A profile of the American eighth grader: NELS: 88 student descriptive summary.* Washington, DC: U.S. Government Printing Office.

5. Richardson, J. L., Dwyer, K., Hansen, W. B., Dent, C., Johnson, C. A., Sussman, S. Y., Brannon, B., & Flag, B. (1989). Substance use among eighth-grade students who take care of themselves after school. *Pediatrics, 84*(3), 556–566.

   Zelnik, M., & Kantner, J. F. (1977). Sexual and contraceptive experience of young unmarried women in the United States, 1976 and 1971. *Family Planning Perspectives 9*, 55-71.

6. U.S. Bureau of the Census. (1994). *More education means higher career earnings.* [Statistical Brief]. Washington, DC: U.S. Department of Commerce.

7. Bennett, C. E. (1995). *The black population in the United States: March 1994 and 1993.* U.S. Bureau of the Census, Current Population Reports, P20–480. Washington, DC: U.S. Government Printing Office.

8. The Alan Guttmacher Institute. (1994). *Sex and America's teenagers.* New York: Author.

9. Strasburger, V. C. (1995). *Adolescents and the media: Medical and psychological impact.* Newbury Park, CA: Sage.

10. Torney-Purta, J. (1990). Youth in relation to social institutions. In S. S. Feldman & G. R. Elliott (Eds.), *At the threshold: The developing adolescent* (pp. 457–477). Cambridge, MA: Harvard University Press.

11. U.S. Bureau of the Census. (1994). *Statistical abstract of the United States, 1994.* Washington, DC: U.S. Government Printing Office.

12. O'Hare, W. P. (1992). America's minorities: The demographics of diversity. *Population Bulletin, 47* (4).

13. Johnston, L. D., O'Malley, P. M., & Bachman, J. G. (1994). *National survey results on drug use from the Monitoring the Future study.* Rockville, MD: National Institute on Drug Abuse.

14. The Alan Guttmacher Institute, 1994.

15. Ibid.

16. U.S. Bureau of the Census, *Statistical abstract,* 1994.

17. U.S. Department of Education, Office of Educational Research and Improvement, National Center for Education Statistics. (1993). *120 years of American education: A statistical portrait*. Washington, DC: U.S. Department of Education.

18. Millstein, S. G., Petersen, A. C., & Nightingale, E. O. (Eds.). (1993). *Promoting the health of adolescents: New directions for the twenty-first century*. New York: Oxford University Press.

19. Suicide among children, adolescents, and young adults—United States, 1980–1992. (21 April 1995). *Morbidity and Mortality Weekly Report, 44* (15), 289–291.

    U.S. Department of Justice, Office of Justice Programs, Bureau of Justice Statistics. (February, 1994). *Firearms and crimes of violence*. NCJ-146844. Washington, DC: U.S. Department of Justice.

20. Hingson, R., & Howland, J. (1993). Promoting safety in adolescents. In S. G. Millstein, A. C. Petersen, & E. O. Nightingale (Eds.), *Promoting the health of adolescents: New directions for the twenty-first century* (pp. 305–327). New York: Oxford University Press.

    Millstein, S. G., & Litt, I. F. (1990). Adolescent health. In S.S. Feldman & G. R. Elliott (Eds.), *At the threshold: The developing adolescent,* (pp. 431–456). Cambridge, MA: Harvard University Press.

21. Dryfoos, J.G. (1990). *Adolescents at risk: Prevalence and prevention*. New York: Oxford University Press.

22. National Research Council. (1993). *Losing generations: Adolescents in high-risk settings*. Washington, DC: National Academy Press.

23. Wilson, W. J. (1993). Poverty, health, and adolescent health promotion. *Promoting adolescent health: Third symposium on research opportunities in adolescence*. Washington, DC: Carnegie Council on Adolescent Development.

24. Brown, S. S., & Eisenberg, L. (Eds.). (1995). *The best intentions: Unintended pregnancy and the well-being of children and families*. Washington, DC: National Academy Press.

25. Lynch, B. S., & Bonnie, R. J. (Eds.). (1994). *Growing up tobacco free: Preventing nicotine addiction in children and youths*. Washington, DC: National Academy Press.

CHAPTER FOUR

Reducing Risks, Enhancing Opportunities: Essential Requirements for Healthy Development

1. Dryfoos, J. G. (1990). *Adolescents at risk: Prevalence and prevention*. New York: Oxford University Press.

2. Donovan, J., & Jessor, R. (1985). Structure of problem behavior in adolescence and young adulthood. *Journal of Consulting and Clinical Psychology, 53,* 890–904.

   Jessor, R., & Jessor, S. L. (1977). *Problem behavior and psychosocial development: A longitudinal study of youth*. New York: Academic Press.

3. Elliott, D. S. (1993). Health-enhancing and health-compromising lifestyles. In S. G. Millstein, A. C. Petersen, & E. O. Nightingale (Eds.), *Promoting the health of adolescents: New directions for the twenty-first century* (pp. 119–145). New York: Oxford University Press.

4. Millstein, S. G., Petersen, A. C., & Nightingale, E. O. (Eds.). (1993). *Promoting the health of adolescents: New directions for the twenty-first century*. New York: Oxford University Press.

5. Hamburg, B. A. (1990). *Life skills training: Preventive interventions for young adolescents*. Washington, DC: Carnegie Council on Adolescent Development.

6. Price, R. H., Cioci, M., Penner, W., & Trautlein, B. (1990). *School and community support programs that enhance adolescent health and education*. Washington, DC: Carnegie Council on Adolescent Development.

7. Nightingale, E. O., & Wolverton, L. (1993). Adolescent rolelessness in modern society. *Teachers College Record, 94,* 472–486.

8. Price, Cioci, Penner, & Trautlein, 1990.

9. Freedman, M. (1993). *The kindness of strangers: Adult mentors, urban youth, and the new volunteerism*. San Francisco: Jossey-Bass.

10. Hamburg, 1990.

11. Hedin, D. (1986). *Students as teachers: A tool for improving school climate and productivity*. Background paper prepared for the Carnegie Forum on Education and the Economy.

12. Hamburg, B. A., & Varenhorst, B. B. (1972). Peer counseling in the secondary schools. *American Journal of Orthopsychiatry, 4,* 566–581.

13. Hedin, 1986.

14. Hamburg, 1990.

15. Ibid.

16. Ibid.

CHAPTER FIVE

Reengaging Families with Their Adolescent Children

1. Princeton Survey Research Associates. *Newsweek-Children's Defense Fund Poll.* Conducted October 18–November 7, 1993.

2. Baumeister, R. F., & Leary, M. R. (1995). The need to belong: Desire for interpersonal attachments as a fundamental human motivation. *Psychological Bulletin, 117,* 497–529.

3. Who's Who among American High School Students. (1995). *A portrait of a generation: 25 years of teen behavior and attitudes.* Lake Forest, IL: Educational Communications, Inc.

   Louis Harris and Associates, Inc. (1989). *Girl Scouts survey on the beliefs and moral values of America's children.* New York: Girl Scouts of the United States of America.

4. Elder, G. J., Jr. (1995). Life trajectories in changing societies. In A. Bandura (Ed.), *Self-efficacy in changing societies* (pp. 46–68). New York: Cambridge University Press.

   Jarrett, R. L. (1995). Growing up poor: The family experiences of socially mobile youth in low-income African American neighborhoods. *Journal of Adolescent Research, 10,* 111-135.

5. Small, S. (1990). *Preventive programs that support families with adolescents.* Washington, DC: Carnegie Council on Adolescent Development.

6. Steinberg, L. (1990). Autonomy, conflict, and harmony in the family relationship. In S. S. Feldman & G. R. Elliott (Eds.), *At the threshold: The developing adolescent* (pp. 255- 276). Cambridge, MA: Harvard University Press.

7. Small, 1990.

8. Zill, N., & Nord, C. W. (1994). *Running in place: How American families are faring in a changing economy and an individualistic society.* Washington, DC: Child Trends, Inc.

9. Epstein, J. L., & MacIver, D. J. (1990). *Education in the middle grades: Overview of national practices and trends.* Columbus, OH: National Middle School Association.

10. Epstein, J. L. (1995). School/family/community partnerships: Caring for the children we share. *Phi Delta Kappan, 76,* 701–712.

11. Small, 1990.

12. Hill, J. P. (1988). Adapting to menarche: Familial control and conflict. In M. R. Gunnar & W. A. Collins (Eds.), *Development during the transition to adolescence: Minnesota symposium on child psychology, Volume 21* (pp. 43–77). Hillsdale, NJ: Lawrence Erlbaum Associates, Inc.

13. Elster, A. B., & Kuznets, N. J. (1994). *AMA guidelines for adolescent preventive services (GAPS): Recommendations and rationale.* Baltimore: Williams & Wilkins.

14. The Carnegie Council's report, *A Matter of Time,* called for partnerships between community programs and families. It cited five constructive ways to involve family members in the work of youth organizations (p. 88).

15. Carnegie Council on Adolescent Development. (1994). *Consultation on afterschool programs.* Washington, DC: Author.

16. Small, 1990.

CHAPTER SIX

Educating Young Adolescents for a Changing World

1. Simmons, R. G., & Blyth, D. A. (1987). *Moving into adolescence: The impact of pubertal change and school context.* Hawthorne, NY: Aldine.

2. Task Force on Education of Young Adolescents. (1992). *Turning points: Preparing American youth for the twenty-first century.* Washington, DC: Carnegie Council on Adolescent Development.

3. Slavin, R. E. (1990). *Cooperative learning: Theory, research, and practice.* Englewood Cliffs, NJ: Prentice-Hall.

   ———. (1991). Synthesis of research on cooperative learning. *Educational Leadership,* 72–83.

   ———. (1994). *Educational psychology: Theory into practice.* 4th ed. Boston: Allyn & Bacon.

4. Scales, P. C., & McEwin, K. (1994). *Growing pains: The making of America's middle school teachers.* Columbus, OH: National Middle School Association.

5. Zill, N., & Nord, C. W. (1994). *Running in place: How American families are faring in a changing economy and an individualistic society.* Washington, DC: Child Trends, Inc.

6. Dryfoos, J. G. (1994). *Full-service schools: A revolution in health and social services for children, youth, and families.* San Francisco: CA: Jossey-Bass.

7. Council of Chief State School Officers. (1992). *Reform in middle grade education: Current status, future directions.* Washington, DC: Author.

Council of Chief State School Officers. (1992). *Turning points states in action: An interim report of the middle grade school state policy initiative.* Washington, DC: Author.

CHAPTER SEVEN

Promoting the Health of Adolescents

1. Klerman, L.V. (1993). The influence of economic factors. In S. G. Millstein, A. C. Petersen, & E. O. Nightingale (Eds.), *Promoting the health of adolescents: New directions for the twenty-first century* (pp. 38–57). New York: Oxford University Press.

   Wilson, W. J. (1993). Poverty, health, and adolescent health promotion. *Promoting adolescent health: Third symposium on research opportunities in adolescence.* Washington, DC: Carnegie Council on Adolescent Development.

2. Millstein, S. G. (1993). A view of health from the adolescent's perspective. In S. G. Millstein, A. C. Petersen, & E. O. Nightingale (Eds.), *Promoting the health of adolescents: New directions for the twenty-first century* (pp. 97–118). New York: Oxford University Press.

   Evans, N., Gilpin, E., Farkas, A. J., Shenassa, E., & Pierce, J. P. (1995). Adolescents' perceptions of their peers' health norms. *American Journal of Public Health, 85,* 1064–1069.

3. Jacobs Quadrel, M., Fischhoff, B., & Davis, W. (1993). Adolescent (in)vulnerability. *American Psychologist, 48,* 102–116.

4. U.S. Congress, Office of Technology Assessment. (1991). *Adolescent Health—Volume III: Cross-cutting issues in the delivery of health and related services.* OTA-H-467. Washington, DC: U.S. Government Printing Office.

5. Hamburg, D. A. (1992). *Today's children: Creating a future for a generation in crisis.* New York: Times Books.

6. Katchadourian, H. (1990). Sexuality. In S. S. Feldman & G. R. Elliott (Eds.), *At the threshold: The developing adolescent* (pp. 330–351). Cambridge, MA: Harvard University Press.

7. Brown, S. S., & Eisenberg, L. (Eds.) (1995). *The best intentions: Unintended pregnancy and the well-being of children and families.* Washington, DC: National Academy Press.

8. Ibid.

9. Task Force on Meeting the Needs of Young Children. (1994). *Starting points: Meeting the needs of our youngest children.* New York: Carnegie Corporation of New York.

10. U.S. Department of Justice, Bureau of Justice Statistics. (1994). *Criminal victimization in the United States, 1992. A national crime victimization survey report.* NCJ-145125. Washington, DC: U.S. Government Printing Office.

11. Elliott, D. S. (1993). Health-enhancing and health-compromising lifestyles. In S. G. Millstein, A. C. Petersen, & E. O. Nightingale (Eds.), *Promoting the health of adolescents: New directions for the twenty-first century* (pp. 119–145). New York: Oxford University Press.

12. Snyder, H. N., & Sickmund, M. (1995). *Juvenile offenders and victims: A focus on violence.* NCJ 153570. Washington, DC: U.S. Department of Justice.

13. Earls, F., Cairns, R. B., & Mercy, J. A. (1993). The control of violence and the promotion of nonviolence in adolescents. In S. G. Millstein, A. C. Petersen, & E. O. Nightingale (Eds.), *Promoting the health of adolescents: New directions for the twenty-first century* (pp. 285–304). New York: Oxford University Press.

    Elliott, 1993.

14. Drug Strategies. (1995). *Keeping score: What we are getting for our federal drug control dollars.* Washington, DC: Author.

15. Johnston, L. D., O'Malley, P. M., & Bachman, J. G. (1994). *National survey results on drug use from the Monitoring the Future study, 1975–1993: Vol. I: Secondary school students.* Washington, DC: U.S. Government Printing Office.

16. Pentz, M. A., Dwyer, J. H., MacKinnon, D. P., Flay, B. R., Hansen, W. B., Wang, E. Y. I., & Johnson, C. A. (1989). A multi-community trial for primary prevention of adolescent drug abuse: Effects on drug use prevalence. *Journal of the American Medical Association, 261,* 3259–3266.

    Elliott, 1993.

17. Botvin, G. J., Baker, E., Dusenbury, L., Botvin, E. M., & Diaz, T. (1995). Long-term follow-up results of a randomized drug abuse prevention trial in a white middle-class population. *Journal of the American Medical Association, 273,* 1106–1112.

18. Ibid.

19. Ibid.

20. Lynch, B. S., & Bonnie, R. J. (Eds.). (1994). *Growing up tobacco free: Preventing nicotine addiction in children and youths*. Washington, DC: National Academy Press.

21. Kandel, D., & Yamaguchi, K. (1993). From beer to crack: Developmental patterns of drug involvement. *American Journal of Public Health, 83,* 851–855.

22. U.S. Department of Health and Human Services. (1994). *Preventing tobacco use among young people: A report of the surgeon general*. Washington, DC: U.S. Government Printing Office.

23. U.S. Congress, Office of Technology Assessment, 1991.

24. Ibid.

25. Kronick, R. (1989). *Adolescent health insurance status: Analyses of trends in coverage and preliminary estimates of the effects of an employer mandate and medicaid expansion on the uninsured*. Background paper, prepared for U.S. Congress, Office of Technology Assessment. Washington, DC: U.S. Government Printing Office.

U.S. Congress, Office of Technology Assessment, 1991.

26. Fox, H. B., & McManus, M. A. (1995). Medicaid managed care: A briefing book on issues for children and adolescents. In M. R. Solloway & P. P. Budetti (Eds.), *Child health supervision: Analytical studies in the financing, delivery, and cost-effectiveness of preventive and health promotion services for infants, children, and adolescents* (pp. 136–168). Arlington, VA: National Center for Education in Maternal and Child Health.

27. U.S. General Accounting Office. (1994). *Health care: School-based health centers can expand access for children*. GAO-HEHS-95-35. Washington, DC: Author.

28. National Institute of Nursing Research. (1993). *Health promotion for older children and adolescents: A report of the NINR priority expert panel on health promotion*. NIH Publication No. 93-2420. Washington, DC: U.S. Department of Health and Human Services.

29. Faigel, H. C., Sznajderman, S., Tishby, O., Turel, M., & Pinus, U. (1995). Attention deficit disorder during adolescence: A review. *Journal of Adolescent Health, 16,* 174–184.

30. U.S. General Accounting Office, 1994.

31. U.S. Congress, Office of Technology Assessment, 1991, p. 45.

32. Brooks-Gunn, J., & Paikoff, R. L. (1993). "Sex is a gamble, kissing is a game": Adolescent sexuality and health promotion. In S.G. Millstein, A.C. Petersen, & E. O. Nightingale (Eds.), *Promoting the health of adolescents: New directions for the twenty-first century* (pp. 180- 208). New York: Oxford University Press.

Moore, K. A., Sugland, B. W., Blumenthal, C., Glei, D., & Snyder, N. (1995). *Adolescent pregnancy prevention programs: Interventions and evaluations*. Washington, DC: Child Trends, Inc.

Brown, S. S., & Eisenberg, L. (Eds.). (1995). *The best intentions: Unintended pregnancy and the well-being of children and families*. Washington, DC: National Academy Press.

CHAPTER EIGHT

Strengthening Communities with Adolescents

1. Timmer, S. G., Eccles, J., & O'Brien, I. (1985). How children use time. In F. T. Juster & F. B. Stafford (Eds.), *Time, goods and well-being*. Ann Arbor: University of Michigan, Institute for Social Research.

Medrich, E. A., & Marzke, C. (1991). *Young adolescents and discretionary time use: The nature of life outside school*. Unpublished manuscript prepared for the Carnegie Council on Adolescent Development, Washington, DC.

2. U.S. Department of Education, Office of Educational Research and Improvement, National Center for Educational Statistics. (1990). *A profile of the American eighth grader: NELS: 88 student descriptive summary*. Washington, DC: U.S. Government Printing Office.

3. Richardson, J. L., Dwyer, K., Hansen, W. B., Dent, C., Johnson, C. A., Sussman, S. Y., Brannon, B., & Flag, B. (1989). Substance use among eighth-grade students who take care of themselves after school. *Pediatrics, 84* (3), 556–566.

4. Oldenburg, R. (1994). *The great good place*. New York: Shooting Star, pp. 262–283.

5. Erickson, J. B. (1991). *1992–1993 Directory of American youth organizations* (4th ed.). Minneapolis: Free Spirit Publishing.

6. U.S. Department of Education, 1990, pp. 50–54.

7. Carnegie Council on Adolescent Development. (1992). *A matter of time: Risk and opportunity in the nonschool hours*. Washington, DC: Author.

8. Carnegie Council on Adolescent Development. (1994). *Consultation on afterschool programs.* Washington, DC: Author.

9. Monks, V. (1994). Giving young people something to say yes to. *Land and people. The Trust for Public Land Annual Report, 6,* 14–19.

10. Carnegie Council on Adolescent Development, 1994.

11. Mayor's Youth Development Task Force. (1994). *Chicago for youth: Blueprints for change.* Chicago: Author.

12. Gardner, J. W. (1992). *Reinventing community.* New York: Carnegie Corporation of New York.

13. U.S. Department of Education, 1990.

14. Carnegie Council on Adolescent Development, 1994.

15. Improved training for youth workers at the community level is the focus of a series of efforts being undertaken by the Academy for Educational Development's (AED) Center for Youth Development and Policy Research. Funded by the DeWitt Wallace-Reader's Digest Fund, AED is assessing the feasibility of a staff development initiative to improve training for youth workers at the community level by generating models and defining the characteristics and benefits of effective coordinated community-based training strategies; creating tools and processes that give communities the capacity to assess their readiness and resources for building coordinated training strategies; creating a national organization or structure that has the capacity to coordinate or deliver information and technical assistance to communities and to champion the idea of community-based staff training; and creating short-term and long-term plans for increasing community capacity. In another effort, which is funded by the U.S. Department of Justice, AED is developing a professional training curriculum program for youth workers in community-based agencies serving high-risk youth.

CHAPTER NINE

Redirecting the Pervasive Power of Media

1. Strasburger, V. C. (1995). *Adolescents and the media: Medical and psychological impact.* Newbury Park, CA: Sage.

2. Ibid.

3. Huston, A. C., Donnerstein, E., Fairchild, H., Feshbach, N. D., Katz, P. A., Murray, J. P., Rubinstein, E. A., Wilcox, B. L., & Zuckerman, D. (1992). *Big world, small screen: The role of television in American society.* Lincoln, NE: University of Nebraska Press.

4. Ibid.

5. Christenson, P. G., & Roberts, D. F. (1990). *Popular music in early adolescence.* Washington, DC: Carnegie Council on Adolescent Development.

   Strasburger, 1995.

6. Keating, D. P. (1990). Adolescent thinking. In S. S. Feldman & G. R. Elliott (Eds.), *At the threshold: The developing adolescent* (pp. 54–89). Cambridge, MA: Harvard University Press.

7. Torney-Purta, J. (1990). Youth in relation to social institutions. In S.S. Feldman & G. R. Elliott (Eds.), *At the threshold: The developing adolescent* (pp. 457–477). Cambridge, MA: Harvard University Press.

8. Dietz, W. H., & Gortmaker, S. L. (1985). Do we fatten our children at the television set? Obesity and television viewing in children and adolescents. *Pediatrics, 75,* 807–812.

9. Brooks-Gunn, J., & Reiter, E. O. (1990). The role of pubertal processes. In S. S. Feldman & G. R. Elliott, (Eds.), *At the threshold: The developing adolescent* (pp. 16–53). Cambridge, MA: Harvard University Press.

10. Strasburger, 1995; Huston et al., 1992.

11. See "Connecting the Media and Adolescent Development Professionals," in this chapter.

12. Huston et al., 1992.

13. Christenson & Roberts, 1990.

14. Bash, A. (1995 July 10). V-chip: Vital part of violence debate. *USA Today,* p. 3D.

15. Lacayo, R. (1995 June 12). Violent reaction. *Time, 145*(24), 24–30.

16. Hobbs, R. (1994). Teaching media literacy—Yo! Are you hip to this? *Media Studies Journal, 8*(4), 135–145.

17. Roberts, D. F., & Maccoby, E. E. (1985). Effects of mass communication. In G. Lindzey & E. Aronson (Eds.), *Handbook of social psychology, volume 2* (pp. 539–598). New York: Random House.

    Bauman, K. E., LaPrelle, J., Brown, J. D., Koch, G. G., & Padgett, C. S. (1991). The influence of three mass media campaigns on variables related to adolescent cigarette smoking: Results of a field experiment. *American Journal of Public Health, 81*(5), 597–604.

    Flora, J. A., Maibach, E.W., & Maccoby, N. (1989). The role of media across four levels of health promotion intervention. *Annual Review of Public Health, 10,* 181–201.

DeJong, W., & Winsten, J. A. (1990). The use of mass media in substance abuse prevention. *Health Affairs, 9,* 30–46.

18. Flora, J. A. (1990). *Strategies for enhancing adolescents' health through music media.* Washington, DC: Carnegie Council on Adolescent Development.

19. The Center for Media Education has launched the Children and the Information Superhighway Project, which will link academic researchers with policy makers to develop "a solid intellectual base for policymaking." In addition, the Project will create a Children's Media Policy Network to monitor the development of information superhighway policy and will produce a quarterly publication, the *Children's Media Policy Bulletin*, which will also be published on line.

EPILOGUE

Looking to the Future: Sustaining the Council's Perspective

1. Carnegie Corporation of New York. (1990). Adolescence: Path to a productive life or a diminished future? *Carnegie Quarterly, 35* (1,2).

   Hamburg, D. A. (1989). *Early adolescence: A critical time for interventions in education and health.* Presidential Essay. New York: Carnegie Corporation of New York.

   Hamburg, D. A. (1986). *Preparing for life: The critical transition of adolescence.* Presidential Essay. New York: Carnegie Corporation of New York.

2. Task Force on Meeting the Needs of Young Children. (1994). *Starting points: Meeting the needs of our youngest children.* New York: Carnegie Corporation of New York.

3. See Appendix B.

4. Task Force on Education of Young Adolescents. (1989). *Turning points: Preparing American youth for the twenty-first century.* Washington, DC: Carnegie Council on Adolescent Development.

5. The American Business Collaboration for Quality Dependent Care is a consortium of corporations that work together to find suitable alternatives for employees who care for children or elderly parents. See "American Businesses Invest in Young Adolescents," in chapter five, for more details.

6. Committee for Economic Development. (1991). *The unfinished agenda: A new vision for child development and education.* New York: Author.

7. The U.S. Department of Health and Human Services recently created the Office of Adolescent Health. Congress passed legislation that enabled the establishment of this office in October 1992.

8. Marshall, R., & Tucker, M. (1992). *Thinking for a living: Education and the wealth of nations.* New York: Basic Books.

9. Snowden, C. (1993). *Preparing teachers for the demands of the twenty-first century: Professional development and the NBPTS vision.* Detroit: National Board for Professional Teaching Standards.

10. American Association for the Advancement of Science. (1989). *Science for all Americans: A project 2061 report on literacy goals in science, mathematics, and technology.* Washington, DC: Author.

11. See Appendix C.

12. Snowden, 1993.

13. In 1987, the American Medical Association established the National Coalition on Adolescent Health to bring together 35 organizations from various disciplines concerned with adolescent health. The coalition is comprised of representatives from the health professions, private foundations, public health associations, and federal agencies that directly affect adolescent health policy. The Coalition has sponsored compendia on adolescent health relating to three topics: tobacco, alcohol, and other drugs; confidential health services; and violence, injury, and abuse.

14. The National Commission on the Role of the School and the Community in Improving Adolescent Health. (1990). *Code blue: Uniting for healthier youth.* Alexandria, VA: National Association of State Boards of Education.

15. Gardner, J. (1994). *American renewal.* New York: Carnegie Corporation of New York.

16. Task Force on Meeting the Needs of Young Children, 1994, p. 95.

17. Falco, M. (1992). *The making of a drug-free America: Programs that work.* New York: Times Books.

18. Chicago Mayor's Youth Development Task Force. (1994). *Chicago for youth: Blueprints for change.* Chicago: Author.

19. Takanishi, R., & Hamburg, D.A. (Eds.). (in press). *Preparing young adolescents for the 21st century: Challenges facing Europe and the United States.* New York: Cambridge University Press.

20. Johann Jacobs Foundation. (1995). *Annual Report, 1995.* Zurich: Author.

ACKNOWLEDGMENTS

▪ ▪

If the Carnegie Council on Adolescent Development is able to leave a rich legacy, it will be due in large measure to the many people who have made a long-term commitment to enhancing the life chances of American adolescents. These individuals have made substantial contributions to the Council's work during the nine years of its existence. In so doing, they have fulfilled the aim of this intersectoral body: to make connections across disciplinary and professional boundaries for the benefit of all young people. It is no easy task to accord each of them the recognition they so well deserve.

We deeply appreciate the efforts of the extraordinary twenty-six members of the Council whose biographical sketches can be found in Appendix D. None of the Council's major reports nor their impact over the years could have been achieved without each of these members. From the outset of this experiment, they have guided all of the Council's initiatives, offered strategic advice on emerging issues that required the Council's involvement, and provided steady leadership in designing and bringing projects to successful fruition.

Some Council members assumed key responsibilities as chairs of its task forces and working groups. David Hornbeck was the chair of the Task Force on Education of Young Adolescents, bringing his continuing passion for education reform to the effort. Billie Tisch co-chaired the Task Force on Youth Development and Community Programs, with Carnegie Corporation Trustee and honorary Council member, James Comer. It was she who had the foresight to urge the Council to focus on the then-unrecognized potential of voluntary, community, and youth organizations in adolescents' lives.

Michael I. Cohen, a leader in the development of adolescent medicine, served as the vice-chair of the Adolescent Health Advisory Panel, which guided a joint project of the Council and the U.S. Congress Office of Technology Assessment (OTA) that resulted in the first national, comprehensive report on adolescent health. Senators Daniel K. Inouye and Nancy Landon Kassebaum, both members of the Council, and a bipartisan group from both houses of Congress had the foresight to initiate the request for this study.

Fred M. Hechinger, the dean of American education writers, produced the Council's publication, *Fateful Choices,* aimed at reaching a general audience about crucial opportunities to promote the health of adolescents. Beatrix A. Hamburg chaired a working group on life skills training during adolescence, which resulted in a major analytical resource on the subject. Eleanor E. Maccoby chaired the Science Policy Working Group, which brought together researchers and federal science administrators to discuss research gaps and opportunities. We are deeply grateful to these members of the Council for their important contributions. We are also thankful to Richard Price, who chaired the Council's Working Group on Social Support Networks.

To sustain the work of the Council between its meetings, a staff working group within the Corporation met on a monthly basis. Over the years, the core group included Vivien Stewart and Elena O. Nightingale, who retired from the Corporation in December 1994. As the major initiatives of the Council changed, the working group also changed to include Susan G. Millstein, an associate director of the Council from 1987 to 1990, and Jane Quinn, project director for the Task Force on Youth Development and Community Programs from 1990 to 1993. From 1994 to 1995, Susan V. Smith joined the working group. We thank our colleagues for their insights and dedication in translating the Council's wise counsel into specific activities.

The special contributions of Vivien Stewart and Elena Nightingale in supporting the Council's efforts through the Corporation's grant making program should be recognized. Under their leadership, follow-up and other grants were made in research syntheses, middle schools reform, adolescent health, substance abuse, and youth violence. Gloria Primm Brown also handled grants related to adolescent health and youth violence, as well as those related to youth organizations and the media.

The Council sponsored two volumes that synthesized research in key areas. Both informed the adolescent health research and promotion initiatives of the National Institutes of Health. Shirley Feldman and Glen Elliott edited *At the Threshold: The Developing Adolescent* on normal adolescent development. Susan G. Millstein, Anne Petersen, and Elena Nightingale co-edited *Promoting the Health of Adolescents: New Directions for the Twenty-First Century*. We are grateful to these editors and to the authors of the chapters for their contributions to identifying research opportunities and stimulating research funding on adolescent development and health. Martha Zaslow was a valued consultant who produced cogent overviews for the Council's research symposia. Their contributions are likely to keep adolescent health and development on the science policy agenda for years to come.

Several members of Carnegie Corporation staff contributed substantial time, energy, and wisdom to the work of the Council and its concluding report. Avery Russell brought her remarkable editorial and writing talents to bear on the earlier versions of the report, as did members of the staff working group. Anthony W. Jackson, who served as the Council's project director for the Task Force on Education of Young Adolescents and now heads the Corporation's grant making program to stimulate implementation of *Turning Points* recommendations, wrote most of the chapter on schools.

Staff of the Carnegie Council were responsible for the program descriptions and charts and graphs of the report. Allyn Mortimer was irreplacable in researching and drafting the descriptions of programs and supervising the development of charts and graphs. It was her energy, attention to all of the details of producing a report, and good humor that kept the Council staff in good spirits throughout. Timothy McGourthy researched and produced the computer-generated graphics for these materials, while being responsible for the administrative support that is essential for the production of a report to flow smoothly. Jenifer Hartnett was the manuscript manager, research assistant, and proofreader. Elliott Milhollin provided office support to all of us. Katharine Beckman secured photographs for the report and as with all previous Council reports was the liaison with the designers during the production process. We are exceedingly grateful to each of the Council staff for their devotion to seeing that every aspect of the report's production was seriously addressed and consistent with high standards.

As in all our Council activities, Carnegie Corporation staff were helpful in maintaining communications with the New York office. We are especially grateful to Jeanne D'Onofrio, Annette Dyer, and Bernadette Michel for forming a human web of support.

We thank the reviewers of several drafts of the report: the members of the Carnegie Council plus Gloria Primm Brown, James Comer, Joy Dryfoos, Delbert Elliott, Mathea Falco, Susan G. Millstein, Kathryn Montgomery, Elena Nightingale, and Jane Quinn. We appreciate very much the generosity of their time and advice that made this report more accurate and well informed.

Special thanks go to Lynne Constantine and Suzanne Scott of Community Scribes for their careful editing of the manuscript under tight timelines. They came through with professional aplomb. As with all of the Council's major reports, Marc Meadows of Meadows Design Office, produced a lively and imaginative design under rigorous deadlines.

The concluding report of the Council was released at a national meeting in Washington, D.C. Julia C. Chill served as conference coordinator for this final convening of the Council, attending to all the details that are required for a successful meeting.

The Council on Adolescent Development has been a nearly decade long activity. Change and continuity in key staff, listed on page 166, naturally occurred. Allyn Mortimer and Katharine Beckman were there when we first opened the Council's offices in Washington in October 1986. They are the trustees of the Council's history. We owe both of them an enormous debt for their commitment, integrity, and behind-the-scenes activity over the years. They are truly the glue that has held the Council's operation together.

Throughout the life of the Council, our families have been an ever constant source of loving support. David would not have met his responsibilities without the unfailing encouragement of Betty, Eric, and Peggy. Ruby thanks Louis L. Knowles and Marika Takanishi Knowles, who became an adolescent during the Council's life, for reminding her about what really counts in all of life's great transitions.

D. A. H.   R. T.
New York, New York   Washington, D.C.

TASK FORCE ON EDUCATION OF YOUNG ADOLESCENTS

CHAIR

David W. Hornbeck
Of Counsel, Hogan and Hartson
Washington, D.C.

MEMBERS

Bill Clinton
Governor
State of Arkansas
Little Rock, Arkansas

James P. Comer
Maurice Falk Professor of
    Child Psychiatry
Yale University
Child Study Center
New Haven, Connecticut

Alonzo A. Crim
Benjamin E. Mays Chair of
    Urban Educational
    Leadership
Department of Educational
    Administration
Georgia State University
Atlanta, Georgia

Jacquelynne Eccles
Professor
Department of Psychology
University of Colorado
Boulder, Colorado

Lawrence W. Green
Vice President
Henry J. Kaiser Family
    Foundation
Menlo Park, California

Fred M. Hechinger
President
New York Times Company
    Foundation, Inc.
New York, New York

Renee R. Jenkins
Associate Professor of Pediatrics
Director of Adolescent Medicine
Howard University School
    of Medicine
Washington, D.C.

Nancy L. Kassebaum
United States Senator
Kansas

Hernan LaFontaine
Superintendent of Schools
Hartford, Connecticut

Deborah W. Meier
Principal
Central Park East Secondary
    School
New York, New York

Amado M. Padilla
Professor
School of Education
Stanford University
Stanford, California

Anne C. Petersen
Dean
College of Health and Human
    Development
Pennsylvania State University
State College, Pennsylvania

Jane Quinn
Director of Program Services
Girls Clubs of America
New York, New York

Mary Budd Rowe
Professor
College of Education
University of Florida
Gainesville, Florida

Roberta Simmons*
Professor of Psychiatry
    and Sociology
University of Pittsburgh
Pittsburgh, Pennsylvania

Marshall S. Smith
Dean
School of Education
Stanford University
Stanford, California

Admiral James D. Watkins**
U.S. Navy, Retired
Washington, D.C.

* *Deceased, 1993.*

**Served as a member of the*
Task Force until his designation
by President Bush as Secretary
of Energy on January 26, 1989.

Titles and affiliations
reflect dates of service
as Task Force members.

TASK FORCE ON YOUTH DEVELOPMENT AND COMMUNITY PROGRAMS

CO-CHAIRS

James P. Comer
Maurice Falk Professor of
    Child Psychiatry
Yale University
Child Study Center
New Haven, Connecticut

Wilma S. Tisch
Chairman of the Board
WNYC Foundation
Member of the Executive
    Committee
United Way of New York City
New York, New York

MEMBERS

Raymond G. Chambers
Chairman
Amelior Foundation
Morristown, New Jersey

Philip Coltoff
Executive Director
The Children's Aid Society
New York, New York

Jane L. Delgado
President and CEO
National Coalition of Hispanic
    Health and Human Services
    Organizations (COSSMHO)
Washington, D.C.

Joy G. Dryfoos
Independent Researcher
Hastings–on–Hudson, New York

Judith B. Erickson
Director of Research Services
Indiana Youth Institute
Indianapolis, Indiana

John W. Gardner
Miriam and Peter Hass
    Centennial Professor of
    Public Service
Stanford University
Stanford, California

William H. Gray III
President
United Negro College Fund
New York, New York

C. Anne Harvey
Director of the Programs
    Division
American Association of
    Retired Persons
Washington, D.C.

Thomas J. Harvey
President
Catholic Charities U.S.A.
Alexandria, Virginia

Leah Cox Hoopfer
Program Director
Extension, Children, Youth,
    and Family Programs
Michigan State University
East Lansing, Michigan

David S. Liederman
Executive Director
Child Welfare League of America
Washington, D.C.

Dagmar E. McGill
Deputy National Executive
    Director
Big Brothers/ Big Sisters of
    America
Philadelphia, Pennsylvania

Milbrey W. McLaughlin
Director, Center for Research
    on the Context of Secondary
    School Teaching
Stanford University
Stanford, California

Thomas W. Payzant
Superintendent
San Diego City Schools
San Diego, California

Federico Peña
President and CEO
Peña Investment Advisors
Denver, Colorado

Karen Johnson Pittman
Director
Center for Youth Development
    and Policy Research
Academy for Educational
    Development
Washington, D.C.

Hugh B. Price
Vice President
The Rockefeller Foundation
New York, New York

Stephanie G. Robinson
Assistant to the Superintendent
    for Funding-Development
    and Special Initiatives
Kansas City School District
Kansas City, Missouri

Timothy Sandos
At-Large Representative
Denver City Council
Denver, Colorado

Christen G. Smith
Executive Director
American Association for
    Leisure and Recreation
Reston, Virginia

Kenneth B. Smith
President
Chicago Theological Seminary
Chicago, Illinois

Judith Torney-Purta
Professor of Human
    Development
University of Maryland
College Park, Maryland

Jo Uehara
Assistant Executive Director for
    Member Association Services
YWCA of the U.S.A.
New York, New York

Roberta Van Der Voort
Executive Director
United Way of King County
Seattle, Washington

WORKING GROUP ON LIFE SKILLS TRAINING

CHAIR

Beatrix A. Hamburg
Professor of Psychiatry and
    Pediatrics
Director of the Division of Child
    and Adolescent Psychiatry
Mount Sinai School of Medicine
New York, New York

MEMBERS

Gilbert Botvin
Associate Professor
Cornell University Medical
    Center
New York, New York

James P. Connell
Associate Professor in Education
    and Psychology
University of Rochester
Rochester, New York

Thomas Cook
Professor
Center for Urban Affairs
Northwestern University
Evanston, Illinois

Martin Covington
Professor of Psychology
University of California,
    Berkeley
Berkeley, California

Baruch Fischhoff
Professor
Department of Social and
    Decision Sciences
Carnegie-Mellon University
Pittsburgh, Pennsylvania

Jane Quinn
Project Director
Carnegie Council on Adolescent
    Development
Washington, D.C.

Joan Schine
Early Adolescent Helper
    Program
National Helpers Network, Inc.
New York, New York

Robert Selman
Professor
Harvard University
Cambridge, Massachusetts

Roger Weissberg
Associate Professor
Department of Psychology
Yale University
New Haven, Connecticut

Renee Wilson-Brewer
Senior Project Director
Center for Health Promotion
    and Education
Education Development
    Center, Inc.
Newton, Massachusetts

*Titles and affiliations
reflect dates of service
as Task Force members.*

WORKING GROUP ON SOCIAL SUPPORT NETWORKS

CHAIR

Richard H. Price
Professor of Psychology
Director
Michigan Prevention Research
    Center
Institute for Social Research
University of Michigan
Ann Arbor, Michigan

MEMBERS

Vanella Crawford
Congress of National Black
    Churches
Washington, D.C.

Beatrix A. Hamburg
Professor of Psychiatry and
    Pediatrics
Director of the Division of Child
    and Adolescent Psychiatry
Mount Sinai School of Medicine
New York, New York

Kenneth Heller
Psychological Clinic
Department of Psychology
Indiana University
Bloomington, Indiana

Judith Musick
Department of Education and
    Social Policy
Northwestern University
Evanston, Illinois

David Olds
General Pediatrics and
    Adolescent Medicine
University of Rochester
Rochester, New York

Karen Rook
Program in Social Ecology
University of California, Irvine
Irvine, California

Robert Selman
Judge Baker Guidance Center
Harvard University
Cambridge, Massachusetts

PUBLICATIONS

REPORTS

A matter of time: Risk and opportunity in the nonschool hours
Task Force on Youth Development and Community Programs. (1992). Washington, DC: Carnegie Council on Adolescent Development. Abridged version and executive summary available free from the Carnegie Council on Adolescent Development.

Fateful choices: Healthy youth for the 21st century
F. M. Hechinger. (1992). New York, NY: Hill and Wang. Executive summary available free from the Carnegie Council on Adolescent Development.

Turning points: Preparing American youth for the 21st century
Task Force on Education of Young Adolescents. (1989). Washington, DC: Carnegie Council on Adolescent Development. Abridged version available free from the Carnegie Council on Adolescent Development.

BOOKS

Adolescence in the 1990s: Risk and opportunity
R. Takanishi (Ed.). (1993). New York, NY: Teachers College Press.

Promoting the health of adolescents: New directions for the twenty-first century
S. G. Millstein, A. C. Petersen, and E. O. Nightingale (Eds.). (1993). New York, NY: Oxford University Press. Executive Summary available free from the Carnegie Council on Adolescent Development.

At the threshold: The developing adolescent
S. S. Feldman and G. R. Elliott (Eds.). (1990). Cambridge, MA: Harvard University Press.

WORKING PAPERS

Consultation on afterschool programs
Carnegie Council on Adolescent Development. (1994).

Schooling for the middle years: Developments in eight European countries
D. Hirsch. (1994).

Promoting adolescent health: Third symposium on research opportunities in adolescence
Carnegie Council on Adolescent Development. (1993).

Depression in adolescence: Current knowledge, research directions, and implications for programs and policy
A. C. Petersen, B. E. Compas, and J. Brooks-Gunn. (1992).*

Violence prevention for young adolescents: The state of the art of program evaluation
S. Cohen and R. Wilson-Brewer. (1991).*

Violence prevention for young adolescents: A survey of the state of the art
R. Wilson-Brewer, S. Cohen, L. O'Donnell, and I. F. Goodman. (1991).*

Adolescent health care decision making: The law and public policy
J. Gittler, M. Quigley-Rick, and M. J. Saks. (1991).

Life-skills training: preventive interventions for young adolescents
B. A. Hamburg. (1990).*

Popular music in early adolescence
P. G. Christenson and D. F. Roberts. (1990).

Preventive programs that support families with adolescents
S. A. Small. (1990).

Risk taking in adolescence: A decision-making perspective
L. Furby and R. Beyth-Marom. (1990).

School and community support programs that enhance adolescent health and education
R. H. Price, M. Cioci, W. Penner, and B. Trautlein. (1990).

*These papers are no longer available from the offices at Carnegie Council. To receive a copy, please contact the Educational Resources Information Center at 1-800-443-3742.

Strategies for enhancing adolescents' health through music media
J. A. Flora. (1990).

Teaching decision making to adolescents: A critical review
R. Beyth-Marom, B. Fischhoff, M. Jacobs, and L. Furby. (1989).

Adolescent rolelessness in modern society
E. O. Nightingale and L. Wolverton. (1988).

The potential of school-linked centers to promote adolescent health and development
S. G. Millstein. (1988).

Preventing abuse of drugs, alcohol, and tobacco by adolescents
M. Falco. (1988).*

Issues in adolescent health: An overview
K. Hein. (1988).

AIDS in adolescence: A rationale for concern
K. Hein. (1988).

COMMISSIONED PAPERS

Reports were commissioned by the Carnegie Task Force on Youth Development and Community Programs and are available by calling the Educational Resources Information Center at 1-800-443-3742.

Adult service clubs and their programs for youth
A. K. Fitzgerald and A. M. Collins.

Building supportive communities for youth: Local approaches to enhancing youth development
R. O'Brien, K. Pittman, and M. Cahill.

Community-based youth services in international perspective
M. Sherraden.

Evaluation of youth development programs (Summary report of the January 1992 Consultation)
Carnegie Council on Adolescent Development.

Funding patterns of non-profit organizations that provide youth development services: An exploratory study
L. W. Stern.

Gender issues in youth development programs
H. J. Nicholson.

Overview of youth recreation programs in the United States
C. Smith.

Overview of youth sports programs in the United States
V. Seefeldt, M. Ewing, and S. Walk.

Professional development of youthworkers (Summary report of the May 1991 Consultation)
Carnegie Council on Adolescent Development.

The quiet revolution: Elder service and youth development in an aging society
M. Freedman, A. C. Harvey, and C. Ventura-Merkel.

Racial, ethnic, and cultural differences in youth development programs
L. A. Camino.

A rationale for enhancing the role of the non-school voluntary sector in youth development
K. Pittman and M. Wright.

A synthesis of the research on, and a descriptive overview of Protestant, Catholic, and Jewish religious youth programs in the United States
K. C. Dean.

What young adolescents want and need from out-of-school programs: A focus report
S. W. Morris & Company.

Young adolescents and discretionary time use: The nature of life outside school
E. Medrich.

OCCASIONAL PAPERS

Adolescent health: Safeguarding a generation at risk
F. M. Hechinger. Based on a speech delivered at the conference "Crossroads: Critical Choices for the Development of Healthy Adolescents," in Washington, DC, April 12–14, 1992, sponsored by Carnegie Corporation of New York and the Carnegie Council on Adolescent Development.

Business and adolescent health: How to succeed by really trying
J. A. Califano. Based on a speech delivered at the conference "Crossroads: Critical Choices for the Development of Healthy Adolescents," Washington, DC, April 12–14, 1992, sponsored by Carnegie Corporation of New York and the Carnegie Council on Adolescent Development.

Reinventing community
J. W. Gardner. Based on a speech delivered at the conference "A Matter of Time: Risk and Opportunity in the Nonschool Hours," Washington, DC, December 10–11, 1992, sponsored by Carnegie Corporation of New York and the Carnegie Council on Adolescent Development.

The case for comprehensive upgrading of American education
O. B. Butler. Based on a speech delivered at the conference "Turning Points: Education in America in the 21st Century," Washington, DC, June 20, 1989.

The education crisis and the future of our economy
R. Marshall. Based on a speech delivered at the conference "Turning Points: Education in America in the 21st Century," Washington, DC, June 20, 1989.

ESSAYS BY DAVID A. HAMBURG, PRESIDENT, CARNEGIE CORPORATION OF NEW YORK

Children of urban poverty: Approaches to a critical american problem
Reprinted from the 1992 Annual Report of Carnegie Corporation of New York.

Early adolescence: A critical time for interventions in education and health
Reprinted from the 1989 Annual Report of Carnegie Corporation of New York.

Preparing for life: The critical transition of adolescence
Reprinted from the 1986 Annual Report of Carnegie Corporation of New York.

CARNEGIE QUARTERLIES

Saving youth from violence, Winter 1994

Turning points revisited: A new deal for adolescents, Spring 1993.

Adolescent health: A generation at risk, Fall 1992.

Adolescence: Path to a productive life or a diminished future? Winter/Spring 1990.

JOURNAL ARTICLES AND COLLABORATIVE WORKS

"Promoting the healthy development of adolescents." S. G. Millstein, E. O. Nightingale, A. C. Petersen, A. M. Mortimer, and D. A. Hamburg. (1993). *Journal of the American Medical Association, 269* (11), 1413–1415.

"Crucial opportunities for adolescent health." D. A. Hamburg. (1993). *Journal of Adolescent Health, 14,* 495–498.

"The urban poverty crisis: An agenda for children and youth." D. A. Hamburg. (1993). *The Western Journal of Medicine, 159,* 692–697.

"The role of social support and social networks in improving the health of adolescents." D. A. Hamburg, E. O. Nightingale, and A. M. Mortimer. (1991). In W. R. Hendee (Ed.), *The health of adolescents,* pp. 526–542. San Francisco: Jossey-Bass Publishers.

"Preparing for life: The critical transition of adolescence." D. A. Hamburg and R. Takanishi. (1989). *American Psychologist, 44* (5), 825–827.

"Facilitating the transitions of adolescence." D. A. Hamburg, E. O. Nightingale, and R. Takanishi. (1987). *Journal of the American Medical Association, 257* (24), 3405–3406.

WITH THE U.S. CONGRESS OFFICE OF TECHNOLOGY ASSESSMENT (1991):

Adolescent health—Volume 1: Summary and policy options. Washington, DC: U.S. Government Printing Office.

Adolescent health—Volume 2: Background and the effectiveness of selected prevention and treatment services. Washington, DC: U.S. Government Printing Office.

Adolescent health—Volume 3: crosscutting issues in the delivery of related services. Washington, DC: U.S. Government Printing Office.

MEETINGS AND WORKSHOPS

SYMPOSIA ON RESEARCH OPPORTUNITIES IN ADOLESCENCE

FOURTH SYMPOSIUM
The Development of Interethnic Group Relations During Childhood and Adolescence, September 1994

THIRD SYMPOSIUM
Promoting Adolescent Health, June 1993

SECOND SYMPOSIUM
Opportunities in the Health and Education of Adolescents, November 1991

FIRST SYMPOSIUM
Opportunities in Adolescent Development, October 1990

MEETINGS IN CONJUNCTION WITH JOHANN JACOBS FOUNDATION, SWITZERLAND

Frontiers in Education: Schools as Health-Promoting Environments, February 1995, Geneva, Switzerland

Frontiers in the Education of Young Adolescents, November 1994, Marbach Castle, Germany

MEETINGS OF THE COUNCIL ON ADOLESCENT DEVELOPMENT

Ninth Council Meeting, October 13, 1995

Eighth Council Meeting, June 24–25, 1993

Seventh Council Meeting, November 14–15, 1991

Sixth Council Meeting, October 15–16, 1990

Fifth Council Meeting, October 12–13, 1989

Fourth Council Meeting, September 29–30, 1988

Third Council Meeting, February 1–2, 1988

Second Council Meeting, June 29–30, 1987

First Council Meeting, January 11–12, 1987

MEDIA LINKAGES: COUNCIL-SPONSORED SPEAKERS AND THEIR TOPICS

Louis Butler, California Tomorrow
Changing Populations, Emerging Audiences
Cosponsor: Women in Film/Film Festival

Peter Christenson, Lewis and Clark College
Children, Teens, and Popular Music
Cosponsor: *Billboard* magazine

James Comer, Yale University Medical School
Education
Cosponsors: Education 1st! and the National Council for Families and Television

Delbert Elliott, Institute of Behavioral Science, University of Colorado
Adolescent Violence and the Media
Cosponsor: Caucus for Producers, Writers, and Directors

David Hayes-Bautista, Chicano Studies Research Center, University of California at Los Angeles
Voices from the Front Lines: Behind the School House Door
Cosponsor: National Council on Families and Television
Changing Audience Demographics
Cosponsor: Education 1st!

Richard Louv, *San Diego Union*
The World of Today's Adolescent
Cosponsor: Academy of Television Arts and Sciences

Eleanor Maccoby, Department of Psychology, Stanford University
Parenting and Co-Parenting before and after Divorce
Cosponsor: National Council on Families and Television

Ray Marshall, Departments of Economics and Public Policy, University of Texas at Austin
The Economic Crisis and Its Impact on Families, Education, and Society
Cosponsor: Show Coalition

Deborah W. Meier, Central Park East Secondary
  School
Turning Points
Cosponsor: National Council on Families and
  Television

Rosemary Lee Potter, middle school teacher and
  author of *Positive Use of Commercial TV for Kids*
Television, the Accidental Educator
Cosponsor: Education 1st!

Donald Roberts, Stanford University, author of
  Popular Music in Early Adolescence
Violence and the Media
Cosponsor: American Film Institute
Popular Music in Early Adolescence
Cosponsor: *Billboard* Magazine
Children, Teens, and Popular Music
Cosponsor: Recording Industry Association of America

Laurence Steinberg, Center for Research in Human
  Development and Education, Temple University
Conflict and Harmony in the Parent-Teen Relationship
Cosponsor: National Council on Families and
  Television

Renee Wilson-Brewer, Violence Prevention Project,
  Education Development Center
Violence and the Media
Cosponsor: American Film Institute
Adolescent Violence and the Media
Cosponsor: Caucus for Producers, Writers, and
  Directors

Linda Wong, California Tomorrow
Minority Education
Cosponsor: National Council on Families and
  Television

COUNCIL WORKSHOPS

Assessing Promising Prevention Interventions: Life
Skills Training Working Group, May 1988, July 1988,
March 1989

Assessing Promising Prevention Interventions: Social
Support Networks Working Group, June 1988, November 1988, February 1989

Supporting Families with Adolescents, September
1988

Consultation on Health Services and Health Promotion in Middle Grade Schools, June 1988

Consultation on School-Linked Adolescent Health
Centers, November 1987

Creating New Television Programs for and about Adolescents, June 1987

Youth at Risk in the Middle Schools, May 1987

Consultation on Adolescent Violence, May 1987

Toward Healthy Adolescent Development: The Potential of Effective Interventions, April 1987

Working with the Media to Promote Healthy Adolescent Development, April 1987

▪ ▪ ▪ ▪ ▪ ▪ ▪ ▪

BIOGRAPHIES OF MEMBERS OF THE COUNCIL

H. Keith H. Brodie

H. Keith H. Brodie is president emeritus of Duke University, where he is the James B. Duke Professor of Psychiatry and Behavioral Sciences, professor of law, and professor of experimental psychology. Before these positions, he was acting provost and chancellor. Dr. Brodie also served as chief of the psychiatry service at Duke University Hospital and as chairman of the university's department of psychiatry. Before his tenure at Duke, he was assistant professor in the department of psychiatry at Stanford University. Among Dr. Brodie's numerous honors and awards is the 1994 William C. Menninger Memorial Award from the American College of Physicians. He has been president and secretary of the American Psychiatric Association and was an associate editor of the *American Journal of Psychiatry*. He is a member of the National Academy of Sciences–Institute of Medicine, where he has chaired a number of committees. Dr. Brodie is a fellow of the Royal College of Psychiatrists as well as of the Royal Society of Medicine. His most recent publication is *AIDS and Behavior: An Integrated Approach* (1994), which he edited with J. D. Auerbach and C. Wypijewska. Dr. Brodie earned an A.B. from Princeton University and an M.D. from Columbia University College of Physicians and Surgeons.

Michael I. Cohen

Michael I. Cohen, chairman of the department of pediatrics at Albert Einstein College of Medicine–Montefiore Medical Center in New York City, was instrumental in the development of adolescent medicine as a medical speciality. Among his numerous honors are the Society for Adolescent Medicine Award for Outstanding Achievement and the Montefiore Medical Center Staff and Alumni Association Distinguished Physician Award. The author of more than one hundred publications, he holds membership in a number of professional societies, including the Society for Developmental and Behavioral Pediatrics; the Eastern Society for Pediatric Research, where he served on the Executive Council; and the National Academy of Sciences–Institute of Medicine. Dr. Cohen's work has focused on the health needs of adolescents. He served as vice-chair of the advisory panel for the U.S. Congress Office of Technology Assessment's landmark study of adolescent health in 1991. He has held lectureships at several universities, including the University of Colorado and Cornell University Medical College. He is a board member for many nonprofit agencies and has served on the editorial and publication advisory boards of a variety of professional publications. Dr. Cohen earned his B.A. and M.D. from Columbia University and was a postdoctoral fellow at Albert Einstein College of Medicine.

Alonzo A. Crim

Alonzo A. Crim is a professor in the department of education and special assistant to the president on college and school partnerships at Spelman College. He was the Benjamin E. Mays Professor of Urban Educational Leadership in the department of educational administration at Georgia State University. As superintendent of the predominantly black and low-income public schools of Atlanta, Georgia, for fifteen years, Dr. Crim introduced many innovative programs that resulted in a dramatic increase in the number of students completing high school and continuing to postsecondary education. One of these innovations was a districtwide requirement of community service for a high school diploma. A widely published educator, Dr. Crim began his career as a seventh- and eighth-grade science and mathematics teacher and later served as a principal and district superintendent in Chicago and superintendent of the Compton, California, Unified School District. His numerous honors and awards include honorary doctorate degrees from Princeton, Harvard, Tuskegee, and Columbia Universities. Dr. Crim earned a B.A. in sociology from Roosevelt College in Chicago, an M.A. in educational administration from the University of Chicago, and an Ed.D. from the Harvard Graduate School of Education.

Michael S. Dukakis

Michael S. Dukakis, former governor of the Commonwealth of Massachusetts, is a visiting distinguished professor in the political science department at Northeastern University in Boston. Governor Dukakis served for two years in the United States Army, spent in part with the support group to the UN delegation to the Military Armistice Commission in Munsan, Korea. He began his political career as an elected town meeting member in Brookline, Massachusetts. Elected chairman of the town's Democratic organization in 1960, he soon won a seat in the legislature and served four terms. Winning the Massachusetts gubernatorial election in 1974, he served one term in office but was defeated in the 1978 state Democratic primary. Governor Dukakis won election again in 1982 and was reelected to an unprecedented third four-year term in 1986. In 1986, his colleagues in the National Governors' Association voted him the most effective governor in the nation. In 1988, Governor Dukakis won the Democratic nomination for the U.S. presidency but was defeated in the general election by George Bush. Since 1991, he has taught courses in the American presidency, public management, health care reform, public policy, and state and local government at Northeastern University. Governor Dukakis earned a B.A. from Swarthmore College and a J.D. from Harvard Law School.

William H. Gray, III

William H. Gray III is president and chief executive officer of the United Negro College Fund (UNCF). As head of America's oldest black higher education assistance organization, Mr. Gray has led the UNCF to new fundraising records. Mr. Gray served in the U.S. Congress from 1978 until 1991. The first African American to chair the House Budget Committee, he was a leading advocate for strengthening America's educational systems. As chairman of the Democratic Caucus and later as majority whip, he was the highest ranking African American ever to serve in Congress. For more than twenty years, Mr. Gray has been pastor of the five-thousand-member Bright Hope Baptist Church in Philadelphia. He has been a faculty member and professor of history and religion at St. Peter's College, Jersey City State College, Montclair State College, Eastern Baptist Theological Seminary, and Temple University. He earned his B.A. from Franklin and Marshall College, a master's degree in divinity from Drew Theological Seminary, and a master's degree in theology from Princeton Theological Seminary. He also has been awarded more than fifty honorary degrees from American colleges and universities.

Beatrix A. Hamburg

Beatrix A. Hamburg is president of the William T. Grant Foundation and professor of psychiatry and pediatrics at the Mount Sinai School of Medicine, where she was director of the division of child and adolescent psychiatry. Her prior professorial appointments were in the psychiatry departments at the Stanford University School of Medicine and Harvard Medical School. Dr. Hamburg has researched normal adolescence, adolescent psychopathology, and endocrine-behavior interactions. She is noted for her work on peer counseling, studies of diabetic children and adolescents, and studies of the health and mental health status of minority populations. Active in public policy and public service in areas that affect children and youth, she is a member of the Public Health Council of the New York State Department of Health and of the New York Governor's Task Force on Life and the Law. She is also a member of the National Advisory Mental Health Council for the National Institute of Mental Health and of the Institute of Medicine of the National Academy of Sciences. Dr. Hamburg earned a B.A. from Vassar College and an M.D. from the Yale University School of Medicine.

David A. Hamburg

David A. Hamburg has been president of Carnegie Corporation of New York since 1983. Formerly, he served as president of the Institute of Medicine of the National Academy of Sciences. He has been a member of the President's Committee of Advisers on Science and Technology since its formation in 1994. For a decade, Dr. Hamburg was on the Advisory Committee on Medical Research of the World Health Organization. He was a trustee and vice chairman of the board of Stanford University, and was a member of the board of The Federal Reserve Bank of New York, where he was also deputy chairman. He serves on the boards of The Rockefeller University; The Mount Sinai Medical Center, New York; The American Museum of Natural History; and The Johann Jacobs Foundation, Zurich. Dr. Hamburg is the author of *Today's Children: Creating a Future for a Generation in Crisis* (1992). He is chairman of the Carnegie Council on Adolescent Development, founder of the Carnegie Commission on Science, Technology and Government, and co-chairman of the Carnegie Commission on Preventing Deadly Conflict. Dr. Hamburg's professorial appointments have included chairmanship of the department of psychiatry and behavioral sciences at Stanford University, Stanford's Reed-Hodgson Professor of Human Biology, and John D. MacArthur Professor of Health Policy at Harvard University. Dr. Hamburg earned his A.B. and M.D. degrees from Indiana University.

David E. Hayes-Bautista

David E. Hayes-Bautista is the director of the Center for the Study of Latino Health at the University of California at Los Angeles, where he is also a professor in the School of Medicine. Dr. Hayes-Bautista began his career directing La Clínica de la Raza in Oakland, California. Since then, he has been affiliated with numerous public and private organizations that promote public health, including the American Public Health Association's Task Force on Latin American Health Workers, the National Center for Health Services Research, and the State of California's Tobacco Education Oversight Committee. Dr. Hayes-Bautista has written numerous articles and books on Latino health policy, demographics, and inner-city youth and co-authored *The Burden of Support*, which examines the role of Latino youth in an aging society. Dr. Hayes-Bautista has received several awards, among them the Hispanic Business Magazine Hispanic Influential Award, the Chicanos for Creative Medicine Humanitarian Award, and the Outstanding Researcher Award from the Chicano/Latino Medical Association of California. He earned a B.A. from the University of California at Berkeley and an M.A. and Ph.D., both in medical sociology, from the University of California's San Francisco Medical Center.

Fred M. Hechinger

Fred M. Hechinger is senior adviser at Carnegie Corporation of New York. As a reporter, columnist, editor, author, and foundation executive, he has devoted much of his career to issues of education and policies affecting children and society. Mr. Hechinger began his career with *The New York Times* as education editor, later becoming deputy editor of the editorial page. He became president of The New York Times Company Foundation and of The New York Times Neediest Cases Fund, and he began writing a weekly column, "About Education." Mr. Hechinger has authored or co-authored with his wife, Grace, a number of books about American education and youth, including *A Better Start* and *Growing Up in America*. He is a former education editor of *Parents' Magazine* and also a former president of the Education Writers Association, from which he has received a number of awards for his writing. Mr. Hechinger received the George Polk Memorial Award, and he holds the British Empire Medal. He joined the staff of Carnegie Corporation after serving on the Corporation's board for six years. Mr. Hechinger attended New York University and City College of New York, from which he was graduated magna cum laude. He undertook graduate studies at the University of London.

David W. Hornbeck

David W. Hornbeck is the superintendent of schools for the school district of Philadelphia. Mr. Hornbeck chaired the Carnegie Council on Adolescent Development's Task Force on Education of Young Adolescents. He has since worked with several jurisdictions nationwide as an education advisor to develop school restructuring processes. As a partner with Hogan & Hartson in Washington, D.C., Mr. Hornbeck worked with private, nonprofit, and government institutions interested in educational restructuring, including the State of Kentucky, whose reform legislation he designed. From 1976 to 1988, Mr. Hornbeck was the state superintendent of schools for Maryland. He also has served as deputy counsel to the governor of Pennsylvania, and as the executive deputy secretary of education for the Commonwealth of Pennsylvania. He currently serves on the advisory boards and on the boards of directors of several organizations devoted to improving education, among them the National Center on Education and the Economy, the Pew Forum on Education Reform, and the Southern Education Foundation. He is chairman of the Children's Defense Fund board of directors. Mr. Hornbeck earned a B.A. and an LL.D. from Austin College, a Diploma in Theology from Oxford University, a B.D. from Union Theological Seminary, and a J.D., *cum laude,* from the University of Pennsylvania Law School.

Daniel K. Inouye

Daniel K. Inouye is the fifth-ranking member of the United States Senate. As a senator, he has championed improved education for all youth and better health care for all Americans. From 1989 to 1994, Senator Inouye was the chairman of the Committee on Indian Affairs and is a leader in advancing the rights of Indian people in the

United States including American Indians and Native Hawaiians. Currently, he is the Committee's vice chairman. He also is a member of the Senate committees on Appropriations; Commerce, Science, and Transportation; and Rules and Administration; and of the Senate Democratic Steering Committee. In World War II, Senator Inouye served in the all–Japanese American 442nd Infantry Regimental Combat Team, the most highly decorated unit of its size in that war. He was discharged an army captain, with a Distinguished Service Cross, Bronze Star, Purple Heart with cluster, and twelve other medals and citations. He began his career as deputy public prosecutor for the City and County of Honolulu. In 1954, he was elected to the Territorial House of Representatives, where he served two consecutive terms, and, in 1958, he was elected to the Territorial Senate. Senator Inouye became Hawaii's first Congressman in 1959, when he was elected to the U.S. House of Representatives. He served in the House until his election to the U.S. Senate in 1962. Senator Inouye earned a B.A. from the University of Hawaii and a J.D. from the George Washington University Law School.

James M. Jeffords

James M. Jeffords, a Republican Senator from Vermont, is the chairman of the Education, Arts, and the Humanities Subcommittee of the Committee on Labor and Human Resources. Senator Jeffords was first elected to Congress in 1975 as a member of the U.S. House of Representatives, where he was a member of the Agriculture Committee and the ranking Republican member on the Education and Labor Committee. Elected to the Senate in 1989, he sits on a number of Senate Committees including Labor and Human Resources, Appropriations, and Energy and Natural Resource. He has devoted his public life to education, health, and environmental issues. Senator Jeffords served on active duty with the U.S. Navy from 1956 to 1959, retiring from the U.S. Naval Reserve as a captain in 1990. He was president of the Young Lawyers Section of the Vermont Bar Association from 1966 to 1968. He received his B.S in international affairs from Yale University in 1956 and his LL.B. from Harvard Law School in 1962.

Richard Jessor

Richard Jessor has been a member of the faculty at the University of Colorado-Boulder for the past forty-three years. He is a professor in the department of psychology and the director of the Institute of Behavioral Science. For the past seven years, Dr. Jessor has directed the MacArthur Foundation Research Network on Successful Adolescent Development among Youth in High-Risk Settings. His areas of research include adolescent and young adult development, the social psychology of problem behavior, and psychosocial aspects of poverty. Dr. Jessor has been consultant to numerous organizations, including the National Institute on Alcohol Abuse and Alcoholism, the National Institute on Drug Abuse, the National Academy of Sciences, Health and Welfare (Canada), and the World Health Organization. He served on the National Research Council Committee on Child Development Research and Public Policy and on the National Academy of Sciences Panel on High-Risk Youth. Dr. Jessor has authored or edited more than one hundred publications, including seven books. His most recent book is *Ethnography and Human Development: Context and Meaning in Social Inquiry* (in press), edited with A. Colby and R. A. Shweder. Dr. Jessor earned his B.A. from Yale University, an M.A. from Columbia University, and a Ph.D. in clinical psychology from Ohio State University.

Helene L. Kaplan

Helene L. Kaplan is Of Counsel to the firm of Skadden, Arps, Slate, Meagher & Flom. She has practiced law for more than twenty-five years. Mrs. Kaplan has served in the not-for-profit sector as counsel or trustee of many scientific, arts, charitable and educational institutions and foundations, including The American Museum of Natural History; The Committee for Economic Development; The Commonwealth Fund; Carnegie Corporation of New York; The J. Paul Getty Trust; The Mount Sinai Hospital, Medical School, and Medical Center; and Barnard College, where she was chairman of the board. She also served as chairman of the Board of Trustees of Carnegie Corporation of New York. She was a member of the U.S. Secretary of State's Advisory Committee on South Africa, and she served on New York Governor Mario Cuomo's Task Force on Life and the Law, which was concerned with the legal and ethical implications of advances in medical technology. Mrs. Kaplan is a director of Chemical Banking Corporation and Chemical Bank, The May Department Stores Company, Metropolitan Life Insurance Company, Mobil Corporation, and NYNEX Corporation. She is a fellow of the American Academy of Arts and Sciences and a member of the American Philosophical Society. Mrs. Kaplan earned her A.B. from Barnard College and a J.D. from New York University.

Nancy Landon Kassebaum

Nancy Landon Kassebaum, a Republican Senator from Kansas, is the chairman of the Committee on Labor and Human Resources. She also is a member of the committees on Foreign Relations and Indian Affairs. The daughter of Alfred M. Landon, governor of Kansas from 1933 to 1937 and the Republican presidential nominee in 1936, she was introduced to politics at an early age. While raising her four children on a farm in Maize, Kansas, Senator Kassebaum was a member of the Maize School Board, Kansas Governmental Ethics Commission, and the Kansas Committee for the Humanities. In 1975, she accepted a position in Washington as an aide to Republican Senator James Pearson of Kansas. In 1978, she was elected to the seat that opened upon Senator Pearson's retirement. Respected as a coalition builder, Senator Kassebaum is serving her third term in the U.S. Senate. An advocate of fiscal responsibility, she is known as a social moderate with strong interests in education and health care. She has also focused her efforts on international affairs, including foreign aid programs and African issues. Senator Kassebaum earned a B.A. in political science from the University of Kansas and an M.A. in diplomatic history from the University of Michigan.

Thomas H. Kean

Thomas H. Kean is president of Drew University and former governor of the State of New Jersey. As university president, he has stressed the primacy of teaching for all faculty, the creative use of technology in the liberal arts, and the growing importance of international education. He created new awards and scholarships for faculty and students. As governor, he instituted a federally replicated welfare reform program and more than thirty education reforms. Governor Kean delivered the keynote address at the 1988 Republican National Convention. He served on the President's Education Policy Advisory Committee under George Bush and as chair of the Education Commission of the States and the National Governors' Association's Task Force on Teaching. Governor Kean is chairman of Educate America and former chairman of the National Environmental Education and Training Foundation. He is on the board of a number of organizations, including Carnegie Corporation of New York, the Robert Wood Johnson Foundation, and United Health Care Corporation. His most recent book is *The Politics of Inclusion*, published by The Free Press. Governor Kean earned a B.A. from Princeton University and an M.A. from Columbia University Teachers College and holds honorary degrees from twenty-five colleges and universities.

Ted Koppel

Ted Koppel, a thirty-one-year veteran of ABC News, is anchor of "Nightline," television's first late-night network news program. As anchor of "Nightline," he is the principal on-air reporter and interviewer. Mr. Koppel also is the program's managing editor. In its fifteenth year on the air, "Nightline" remains an innovation in broadcast news. Mr. Koppel also has worked as a foreign and domestic correspondent and as bureau chief for ABC News. He has won every major broadcasting award, including twenty-three Emmy Awards, five George Foster Peabody Awards, eight duPont-Columbia Awards, nine Overseas Press Club Awards, two George Polk Awards, and two Sigma Delta Chi Awards, the highest honor bestowed for public service by the Society of Professional Journalists. He recently received the Goldsmith Career Award for Excellence in Journalism by the Joan Shorenstein Barone Center on the Press, Politics and Public Policy at Harvard University. He has received fifteen honorary degrees. Mr. Koppel co-authored the bestseller *In the National Interest* with Marvin Kalb, formerly of CBS News. Mr. Koppel earned a B.A. from Syracuse University and an M.A. in mass communications research and political science from Stanford University.

Hernan LaFontaine

Hernan LaFontaine is professor of administration and supervision in the educational leadership department of the Graduate School of Education at Southern Connecticut State University. As a former science teacher and principal in the New York City schools and later as the head of the Office of Bilingual Education at the New York City Board of Education, Mr. LaFontaine was instrumental in establishing bilingual education in the city. In 1979, Mr. LaFontaine assumed the post of superintendent of schools for the Hartford public school system, where he led major efforts to improve the conditions of the school system. As superintendent, he sought to improve standardized achievement test scores, institute a citywide standardized curriculum, and establish a comprehensive computer-based education program. He actively consulted with parents, community, and business through groups he established early in his tenure, such as the Parents Association President's group and the School/Business Collaborative. Mr. LaFontaine has served as a consultant on bilingual education to the federal Office of Education, the New York Department of Education, and many school systems. He has taught as an adjunct professor at Fordham and New York Universities and has lectured widely throughout the United States. Mr. LaFontaine earned B.S. and M.A. degrees from City College of New York and a Professional Diploma in Education Administration from Fordham University.

Eleanor E. Maccoby

Eleanor E. Maccoby is Barbara Kimball Browning Professor of Psychology Emerita at Stanford University, where she has been on the faculty since 1958. Her primary field of interest is the development of children's social behavior, particularly as it relates to family functioning and child-rearing methods. She is the co-author (with R.H. Mnookin) of *Dividing the Child: The Social and Legal Dilemmas of Custody*, for which she was awarded the William J. Goode Award from the American Sociological Association in 1993, and is the author of *Social Development: Psychological Growth and the Parent-Child Relationship*, in addition to numerous articles and monographs. Dr. Maccoby is the recipient of several distinguished awards in her field, among them the American Psychological Association Award for Distinguished Scientific Contribution and the Kurt Lewin Memorial Award from the Society for the Psychological Study of Social Issues. A pioneer in the psychology of sex differences, Dr. Maccoby was elected to the National Academy of Sciences in 1993. She has been a member of the Institute of Medicine since 1977 and of the American Academy of Arts and Sciences since 1974. Dr. Maccoby earned a B.S. from the University of Washington, where she was elected to Phi Beta Kappa. She earned an M.A. and Ph.D. in psychology from the University of Michigan.

Ray Marshall

Ray Marshall is the Audre and Bernard Rapoport Centennial Chair in Economics and Public Affairs at the Lyndon B. Johnson School of Public Affairs at the University of Texas at Austin. The author or co-author of more than thirty books and monographs and 175 articles, Dr. Marshall has done extensive research on the economics of education, minority business development programs, school-to-work transitions, workplace learning systems, and private pension reform, among other topics. Dr. Marshall, who was U.S. Secretary of Labor under President Jimmy Carter, has received several distinguished honors, among them the Sullivan Distinguished Service Award, the Sydney Hillman Book Award (for *Thinking for a Living*), and the Lewis-Murray-Reuther Social Justice Award from the AFL-CIO Industrial Union Department. Dr. Marshall was a Fulbright Research Professor in Finland and has been a fellow at The Rockefeller Foundation, Harvard University, and the Ford Foundation. He was Wayne Morse Chair in Law and Public Policy at the University of Oregon. Dr. Marshall earned a B.A. in economics and business administration from Millsaps College, an M.A. in economics from Louisiana State University, and a Ph.D. in economics from the University of California at Berkeley.

Julius B. Richmond

Julius B. Richmond is John D. MacArthur Professor of Health Policy Emeritus in the division for health policy research and education at Harvard Medical School. Dr. Richmond directed Head Start in the program's early years. As assistant secretary for health in the U.S. Department of Health and Human Services and Surgeon General of the United States Public Health Service during the Carter administration, he directed the publication of "Healthy People: The Surgeon General's Report on Health Promotion and Disease Prevention." Dr. Richmond has served as chair of the pediatrics department and dean of the medical school at the State University of New York at Syracuse. He also was a professor of child psychiatry and human development at Harvard Medical School and became the director of the Judge Baker Guidance Center and chief of psychiatry at Children's Hospital in Boston. Dr. Richmond's published work spans pediatrics, child health, child development, and public health policy. He has received several distinguished awards, including the Aldrich Award of the American Academy of Pediatrics, the Howland Award of the American Pediatric Society, the Gustave Lienhard Award of the Institute of Medicine, and the Sedgwick Medal of the American Public Health Association. Dr. Richmond earned an M.S. and an M.D. from the University of Illinois at Chicago.

Frederick C. Robbins

Frederick C. Robbins, University Professor Emeritus at Case Western Reserve University and dean emeritus of the Case Western Reserve University School of Medicine, currently is the director of the Center for Adolescent Health at Case Western. With Dr. John Enders and Dr. Thomas Weller, Dr. Robbins received the 1954 Nobel Prize in Physiology and Medicine for the development of techniques for the growth of poliovirus in cultures of nonnervous tissue. Dr. Robbins was director of the department of pediatric and contagious diseases at Cleveland City Hospital. During World War II, he served as the U.S. Army's chief of the virus and rickettsial disease section of the Fifteenth General Medical Laboratory. Dr. Robbins is a charter member of the Technology Assessment Advisory Committee of the U.S. Office of Technology Assessment and was president of the Institute of Medicine of the National Academy of Sciences. He currently serves on the Board of International Health of the Institute of Medicine and co-chairs the Vaccine Action Program between the United States and India. He received the Abraham Flexner Award for Medical Education from the Association of American Medical Colleges. Dr. Robbins earned a B.A. from the University of Missouri, completed a two-year program at the University of Missouri School of Medicine, and earned an M.D. from Harvard Medical School.

Kenneth B. Smith

Kenneth B. Smith is president and associate professor of ministry at the Chicago Theological Seminary and an ordained minister of the United Church of Christ. Reverend Smith was a senior minister at the Church of the Good Shepherd in Chicago for sixteen years before he assumed the presidency at the seminary. During his tenure at the Church of the Good Shepherd, the congregation initiated programs in preschool education, after-school care and recreation, nutritional and recreation programs for retired persons, and a program for adolescents with special needs. Reverend Smith currently serves on several local and national voluntary boards and committees, including the board of trustees of National Youth Advocates and the United Way of Chicago. From 1980 to 1981, he was president of the Chicago Board of Education. Among numerous awards, he has received the Educational Award from Operation PUSH and the Humanitarian Award from the Plano Chicago Development Center. His publications include the *Lenten Book of Meditation* and *The United Church of Christ—Issues in Its Quest for Denominational Identity*, edited with Dorothy C. Bass. Reverend Smith earned a B.A. from Virginia Union University in Richmond, Virginia, and a Bachelor of Divinity from Bethany Theological Seminary in Oak Brook, Illinois.

Wilma S. Tisch

Wilma S. Tisch, a civic leader, is chairman emeritus of the board of WNYC (New York Public Broadcasting). She is a trustee of the United Way of New York City, as well as a member of its executive committee. She is vice president of the Jewish Communal Fund; trustee of the Federation of Jewish Philanthropies of New York; member of the Council of Advisors, Hunter College School of Social Work; a trustee of Carnegie Corporation of New York; and a member of the American Jewish Joint Distribution Committee. Ms. Tisch was president of the Federation of Jewish Philanthropies of New York and was vice president of the Council of Jewish Federations. She also is a former trustee of Blythedale Children's Hospital. In 1993, she was a member of the Mayor's Transition Advisory Council, New York City. Ms. Tisch received the Louis D. Marshall Medal from the Jewish Theological Seminary and an honorary Doctor of Humane Letters from Skidmore College and from the Mount Sinai School of Medicine of the City University of New York. Brandeis University named her Milender Fellow in 1981. Born in Asbury Park, New Jersey, Ms. Tisch earned a B.S. from Skidmore College.

P. Roy Vagelos

P. Roy Vagelos is chairman of the board of Regeneron Pharmaceuticals Inc. and former chairman of the board and chief executive officer of Merck & Company, Inc. An authority on lipids and enzymes, Dr. Vagelos began his career as a researcher at the National Institutes of Health, where he became head of the section on comparative biology. He joined the faculty of Washington University in St. Louis, Missouri, and became chairman of the department of biological chemistry of the school of medicine. He later served as director of the university's division of biology and biomedical sciences. Dr. Vagelos held several research and business positions in twenty years at Merck & Company, Inc. The author of more than one hundred scientific papers, Dr. Vagelos received the Enzyme Chemistry Award of the American Chemical Society. He is a member of the National Academy of

Sciences, the American Academy of Arts and Sciences, and the American Philosophical Society. He is chairman of the board of trustees of the University of Pennsylvania and a trustee of The Danforth Foundation. Dr. Vagelos earned an A.B. from the University of Pennsylvania, where he was elected to Phi Beta Kappa, and an M.D. from the College of Physicians and Surgeons of Columbia University.

James D. Watkins

James D. Watkins, retired admiral of the U.S. Navy, is founder and president of the board of governors of Consortium for Oceanographic Research and Education (CORE). He is president of the board of governors of the Joint Oceanographic Institutions (JOI) Inc. Under President George Bush, Admiral Watkins served as Secretary of Energy. He has worked throughout his career to improve the education of young people, especially in mathematics and science. Admiral Watkins served as chairman of the Federal Coordinating Council for Science, Engineering, and Technology's Committee on Education and Human Resources, which produced the first federal government-wide strategic plan for mathematics and science education programs. Admiral Watkins served as chairman of the Presidential Commission on the Human Immunodeficiency Virus (AIDS) Epidemic under President Ronald Reagan. His naval career was capped by his assignment as Chief of Naval Operations. His military decorations include several Distinguished Service and Legion of Merit medals and the Bronze Star. Admiral Watkins is member of the Knights of Malta, an international order of leading Catholic laymen dedicated to humanitarian service and a trustee of Carnegie Corporation of New York. Admiral Watkins is a graduate of the U.S. Naval Academy, earned an M.S. in mechanical engineering from the U.S. Naval Post-Graduate School, and is a graduate of the reactor engineering course at the Oak Ridge National Laboratory.

William Julius Wilson

William Julius Wilson is the Lucy Flower University Professor of Sociology and Public Policy and the director of the Center for the Study of Urban Inequality at the University of Chicago. Professor Wilson is noted for his work on urban poverty and issues of race. He is author of *Power, Racism, and Privilege: Race Relations in Theoretical and Sociohistorical Perspectives*; *The Declining Significance of Race: Blacks and Changing American Institutions*, and *The Truly Disadvantaged: The Inner City, The Underclass, and Public Policy*. A MacArthur Prize Fellow, Professor Wilson is a past fellow at the Center for Advanced Study in the Behavioral Sciences at Stanford University. He is past president of the Consortium of Social Science Associations and of the American Sociological Association. Professor Wilson is a fellow of the American Academy of Arts and Sciences and of the American Association for the Advancement of Science and is a member of the National Academy of Sciences, American Philosophical Society, and National Academy of Social Insurance. Among many awards and honorary degrees, he received the Burton Gordon Feldman Award, given for outstanding contributions in the field of public policy from the Brandeis University Gordon Public Policy Center. Professor Wilson earned a B.A. from Wilberforce University, an M.A. from Bowling Green State University, and a Ph.D. in sociology/anthropology from Washington State University.

■ ■ ■ ■ ■ ■ ■ ■

INDEX OF PROGRAMS CITED IN THE REPORT

Children's Aid Society
105 East 22nd Street
New York, NY 10010
Contact: Philip Coltoff,
Executive Director
Telephone: (212) 949-4917
Fax: (212) 460-5941
Page 82

CityYouth
Constitutional Rights
Foundation
601 South Kingsley Drive
Los Angeles, CA 90005
Contact: Eleanor Kim, Associate
Director
Telephone: (213) 487-5590
Fax: (213) 386-0459
Pages 109, 111

The Congress of National
Black Churches, Inc. /
Project SPIRIT
1225 Eye Street, N.W., Suite 750
Washington, DC 20005-3914
Contact: B.J. Long, Acting
Project Director
Telephone: (202) 371-1091
Fax: (202) 371-0908
Pages 109, 112

Girl Scouts of the USA
420 Fifth Avenue
New York, NY 10018-2202
Contact: Mary Rose Main,
National Executive Director
Telephone: (212) 852-8000
Fax: (212) 852-6517
Page 119

Girls, Inc.
30 East 33rd Street
New York, NY 10016
Contact: Isabel Carter Stewart,
National Executive Director
Telephone: (212) 689-3700
Fax: (212) 683-1253
Page 119

Human Biology Middle Grades
Life Science Curriculum
HUMBIO Curriculum
Program in Human Biology
Department of Biological
Sciences
Building 80-2160

Stanford University
Stanford, CA 94305
Contact: H. Craig Heller
Telephone: (415) 723-1509
Fax: (415) 725-5356
Pages 78, 79

Mediascope
12711 Ventura Boulevard, Suite 250
Studio City, CA 91604
Contact: Marcy Kelly, President
Telephone: (818) 508-2080
Fax: (818) 508-2088
Pages 119, 120, 121

National Helpers Network, Inc.
(Early Adolescent Helper
Program)
245 Fifth Avenue, Suite 1705
New York, NY 10016-8728
Contact: Alice L. Halsted,
President
Telephone: (212) 679-2482
Fax: (212) 679-7461
Pages 109, 111

National Coalition of Hispanic
Health and Human Service
Organizations (COSSMHO)
1501 16th Street, N.W.
Washington, DC 20036
Contact: Jane L. Delgado,
President and Chief Executive
Officer
Telephone: (202) 387-5000
Fax: (202) 797-4353
Page 109

National 4-H Council
7100 Connecticut Avenue
Chevy Chase, MD 20815
Contact: Richard Sauer,
President
Telephone: (301) 962-2820
Fax: (301) 961-2894
Page 106

National Network of Violence
Prevention Practitioners
Education Development Center
55 Chapel Street
Newton, MA 02160
Contact: Gwendolyn J.
Dilworth, Project Coordinator
Telephone: (617) 969-7100
Fax: (617) 244-3436
Page 96

National Urban League
500 East 62nd Street
New York, NY 10021
Contact: Hugh B. Price,
President and CEO
Telephone: (212) 310-9000
Fax: (212) 755-2140
Page 109

Quantum Opportunity
Program
1415 North Broad Street
Philadelphia, PA 19122
Contact: Debbie Scott, Office of
National Literacy Programs
Telephone: (215) 236-4500
Fax: (215) 236-7480
Pages 56, 57

School-Based Youth Services
Program
New Jersey Department of
Human Services
222 South Warren Street
Trenton, NJ 08625-0700
Contact: Edward Tetelman,
Director, Office of Legal and
Regulatory Affairs
Telephone: (609) 292-1617
Fax: (609) 984-7380
Pages 51, 52

YMCA of the USA
101 North Wacker Drive
14th Floor
Chicago, IL 60606-7386
Contact: David Mercer, National
Executive Director
Telephone: (312) 977-0031
Fax: (312) 977-9063
Page 106

YWCA of the USA
726 Broadway
New York, NY 10003
Contact: Prema Mathai-Davis,
National Executive Director
Telephone: (212) 614-2821
Fax: (212) 979-6829
Page 106

STAFF

Ruby Takanishi
Executive Director

Allyn M. Mortimer
Program Associate

Katharine Beckman
Office Administrator

Julia C. Chill
Program/Administrative
    Assistant

Timothy J. McGourthy
Program/Administrative
    Assistant

Wanda M. Ellison
Administrative Assistant

Jenifer Hartnett
Staff Assistant

Elliott Milhollin
Office Clerk

FORMER STAFF

Winnie Bayard
Project Assistant, 1990–93

Bronna Clark
Administrative Secretary,
    1986–89

Annette Dyer
Administrative Assistant,
    1988–91

Anthony W. Jackson
Project Director
Task Force on Education of
    Young Adolescents,
    1987–90

Susan G. Millstein
Associate Director, 1987–90

Elena O. Nightingale
Senior Advisor to the Council,
    1986–94

Jane Quinn
Project Director
Task Force on Youth
    Development and Community
    Programs, 1990–93

Linda L. Schoff
Program/Administrative
    Assistant, 1991–94

Andrea Solarz
Program Associate, 1988–90

CREDITS

PHOTOGRAPHS

Cover: © 1992 Eli Reed, Magnum Photos, Inc.

Page 1: © 1988 Danny Lyon, Magnum Photos, Inc.

Page 8: © Harold Feinstein

Page 18: © 1992 Maria Bastone

Page 26: © Harold Feinstein

Page 33: Mary Ellen Mark/Library

Page 34: © 1985 Ferdinando Scianna, Magnum Photos, Inc.

Page 48: © Maria Bastone

Page 57: © Eric Futran

Page 62: © Eric Futran

Page 74: © Eric Futran

Page 77: © 1994 Leonard Freed, Magnum Photos, Inc.

Page 83: © 1993 Jane Hoffer for National Helpers Network

Page 87: © Maria Bastone

Page 90: © 1992 Maria Bastone

Page 103: © Lee G. Day for Children's Aid Society

Page 104: © 1992 Maria Bastone

Page 111: © 1993 Jane Hoffer for National Helpers Network

Page 112: © Eric Futran

Page 114: © Eric Futran

Page 124: © 1992 Eli Reed, Magnum Photos, Inc.

Page 146: © Eric Futran

QUOTES AND POEMS

Page 17: *Voices from the future: Our children tell us about violence in America,* by Children's Express, edited by Susan Goodwillie (p. 141). New York: Crown Publishers, Inc., 1993.

Page 55: *Kids' voices count: Illuminating the statistics*, by Children's Express Foundation, Inc., edited by Jessica Beels (p. 7). Washington, DC: Author, 1994.

Page 61: "Southern California voices: A forum for community issues," Los Angeles *Times*, May 16, 1995.

Page 67: *Voices from the future: Our children tell us about violence in America*, by Children's Express, edited by Susan Goodwillie (pp. 44-45). New York: Crown Publishers, Inc., 1993.

Page 106: *Kids' voices count: Illuminating the statistics*, by Children's Express Foundation, Inc., edited by Jessica Beels (p. 11). Washington, DC: Author, 1994.

Page 168: "Southern California voices: A forum for community issues," Los Angeles *Times*, May 16, 1995. *Note: the author's full name could not be used because he is an incarcerated minor.*

The world's blind, neglecting its land.

The human race has turned on itself,
destruction's loud

but the world's deaf!

Change can be found if it's truly being
searched for; we as one need to communicate,
guide our youth,

because what we do today is setting the
path for our children!

GEORGE T., 17